PLANT-BASED INSTANT POT COOKBOOK

Plant-Based Instant Pot Cookbook

80 Whole Food, Plant-Based Diet Recipes Made Quick and Easy

Felicia Slattery

Photography by Hélène Dujardin

ROCKRIDGE PRESS

For general information on our other products and services or to obtain technical support, please contact our Customer Care Department within the United States at (866) 744-2665, or outside the United States at (510) 253-0500.

Rockridge Press publishes its books in a variety of electronic and print formats. Some content that appears in print may not be available in electronic books, and vice versa.

Interior and Cover Designer: Erik Jacobsen
Art Producer: Hannah Dickerson
Editor: Marjorie DeWitt
Production Editor: Sigi Nacson
Production Manager: Holly Haydash

Photography © 2021 Hélène Dujardin; food styling by Anna Hampton
Author photo courtesy of Lori Santoro

ISBN: 978-1-64876-397-7
eBook 978-1-64876-398-4
R0

This book is dedicated to my husband, Brent, and our daughters, Grace and Miranda. Thank you for being my taste testers and willing participants in my plant-based home-cooking journey. I love you all!

P.S. Dinner is ready soon, so let's get the table set, girls.

Contents

Introduction

I have a confession to make.

When the Instant Pot came out in 2010 and suddenly became *the* hot new kitchen tool, I wasn't very interested. Before I knew it, my social media timeline was flooded with photos of my friends proudly displaying their Instant Pot creations and waxing poetic over its virtues and, admittedly, I became curious. Finally, a few years later, I decided to see what all the fuss was about and purchased an Instant Pot for myself.

The first recipe I tried cooking in it was a total flop, and the Instant Pot was relegated to the back of a closet for more than a year, until one night when my family was asking for dinner and I had no idea what to make. I remembered the Instant Pot, made a delicious meal that was ready in a snap, and my family loved it.

The Instant Pot is a fabulous appliance, and now I use it all the time. No matter what your experience is with it, I'm confident this book will have all the instructions you need to enjoy delicious plant-based meals from your Instant Pot.

I've been dabbling with a plant-based diet since the mid-1990s, when I first quit dairy and noticed my seasonal allergies disappeared. In those days, finding alternatives was not as easy as it is today, and it wasn't until 2019 that I finally went all-in on a plant-based diet. A doctor had suggested it to help with some digestion problems I was experiencing. After learning about the science behind the diet, I was hooked.

People come to the plant-based diet for many reasons. Whatever your reason is and no matter how long you've been a plant-based eater or an Instant Pot user, you will find the recipes in this book easy to follow and made with accessible ingredients. I hope this book inspires many plant-based Instant Pot family meals to come!

Creamy Spaghetti Squash with Spinach, Olives, and Roasted Red Peppers, page 92

CHAPTER 1
Plant-Based Cooking with the Instant Pot

Welcome to the perfectly delicious marriage of enjoying a healthy plant-based diet and cooking with the almost-like-magic Instant Pot! In this chapter, I'll break down what a plant-based diet involves and share some tips, techniques, and terminology you'll need to know to get the most out of your Instant Pot.

Making the Plant-Based Diet Connection

I don't know about you, but it seems like each time I go to the grocery store, I see more products labeled as "plant-based." Every day, there are new stories about the benefits of a plant-based diet, as well as news that big companies—even well-known brands that produce meat and dairy products—are also jumping on the plant-based bandwagon. It feels like a plant-based revolution, and I couldn't be more excited about it!

Why the reason for the change? It seems more doctors, nutritionists, and other medical professionals, as well as the general public, are finally learning what those who have promoted a whole food, plant-based diet for decades have been screaming from the rooftops: The plant-based diet is an excellent method of eating for human beings.

Like a vegan diet, the core of a plant-based diet involves eating foods that come from plants: fruits, vegetables, grains, beans, legumes, nuts, and seeds. However, many people who follow a vegan lifestyle go beyond what they eat and additionally avoid using animal products of any kind, such as leather and fur in clothing and accessories.

The term "plant-based diet" itself can lead to some confusion, because each person who eats a plant-based diet can have their own definition, and some people even consider themselves as eating a plant-based diet while still consuming some animal products. Rest assured, the meals in *The Plant-Based Instant Pot Cookbook* are 100 percent free of animal products and heavily processed ingredients. There is also minimal use of salt, oils, and refined sugars throughout the recipes in this book—what is known as "SOS-free" in the plant-based diet world.

The Wide World of Plant-Based Eating

Your reasons for eating plant-based food are unique to you, but people generally choose to follow a plant-based diet for health, lifestyle, environmental, and/or ethical reasons. Here are the main approaches to eating this way:

Plant-based: Plant-based eating focuses on foods that are derived from plants. In addition to fruits, veggies, grains, beans, legumes, nuts, and seeds, this can include various plant-based meat, dairy, and egg alternatives and other processed foods that contain no animal products.

Whole food, plant-based (WFPB): This term, first coined by Dr. T. Colin Campbell, author of *The China Study*, refers to eating whole foods as close to their original source as possible while also including small amounts of minimally processed salt, oils, and sugars. Condiments devoid of animal products, such as commercially available gluten-free vegan Worcestershire sauce, are often used to add flavor.

Whole food, plant-based, no salt, oil, or sugar (WFPBSOS-free): Going one step further, this diet eliminates the use of all salt, oils, and refined sugars. Therefore, even minimally processed products, such as hot sauce, are not included because they often contain salt, oil, sugar, or all three.

In this book, the emphasis is on whole food, plant-based recipes, and most recipes are also compliant with a WFPBSOS-free diet. I often list salt as an optional ingredient, which you can always omit if you're following an SOS-free diet.

Benefits of a Plant-Based Diet

The more I learn about the effects of eating a plant-based diet, the more convinced I am of its many benefits. Here are just a few of them:

Weight loss/management: When you eat a nutrient-dense whole food, plant-based diet, you can satisfy your appetite with fewer calories. The beauty of this way of eating is that there is generally no restriction to eating any type of whole food. Eat all the fresh fruits, vegetables, grains, beans, and legumes you want. If you've hit a plateau, you may find limiting dried fruit, nuts, and seeds to one serving per day will help you get back on track.

Reduction of inflammation: Part of the body's built-in defense mechanisms, inflammation is the body's way of eliminating harmful substances. In recent years, chronic inflammation has been associated with cardiovascular diseases, cancer, diabetes, arthritis, joint diseases, and allergies. Eating a plant-rich diet has been shown to reduce inflammation, and may help reverse chronic health issues such as heart disease, high cholesterol, and diabetes.

Immune-boosting properties: Surprisingly, 70 to 80 percent of the immune system is based in your gut microbiome, which is influenced by what you eat. A high-fiber, plant-based diet helps keep your gut, and therefore your immune system, running at optimal levels. A strong immune system not only allows your body to more effectively attack viruses, but it can also reduce your risk for cancer by fighting mutations in your cells before they develop into diseases.

Environmental impact: Eating a plant-based diet is not only good for our health but also for the health of the planet. By eliminating meat and milk from our diets, we can save water and keep it cleaner, reduce greenhouse gas emissions, and protect land from habitat destruction.

Animal welfare: My friend and colleague Kathleen Gage, best-selling author and host of the podcast *Plant Based Eating for Health*, talks about how, prior to eating a plant-based diet, she never made the connection between the animals she regularly rescued on her small Oregon farm and the animals on her plate. For her and many others who enjoy a plant-based diet, compassion for animals is every bit as important as health reasons. Large factory farms are notorious for mistreating animals, and eating a plant-based diet decreases the demand for these inhumane farms.

Building Blocks of the Plant-Based Diet

The building blocks of a plant-based diet are simple: eat fruits, vegetables, beans, legumes, nuts, and seeds, and create meals that have a healthy balance of fat, protein, and carbohydrates high in nutrient density. Avoid highly processed items loaded with salt, oils, and sugars, and what I refer to as "franken-foods": foods you couldn't possibly make in your own kitchen because of the added chemicals and ingredients that are not available to regular people. It's important to note that taking a supplement containing vitamin B_{12} is highly recommended for those eating a 100 percent plant-based diet.

Whole Foods

In a whole food, plant-based diet, all your calories, vitamins, minerals, fiber, fat, protein, and carbs come directly from plant foods. The beauty of eating this way is you don't have to focus on including foods for one nutrient alone, such as more beans for protein or more greens for calcium. If you eat a variety of whole plant foods every day, you are almost guaranteed to reach your daily nutrient requirements.

If you can both find and afford organic plant-based foods, so much the better. But if your budget is more limited, another great thing about eating a plant-based diet is there is nothing more economical than eating grains, greens, and beans! If you are concerned about pesticides, look for the Dirty Dozen list published by the nonprofit Environmental Working Group each year, and avoid those foods especially. Conversely, their Clean Fifteen list is made up of nonorganic foods that are considered safe to buy.

You can also buy frozen or canned whole foods (look for no salt, oil, or sugar added) for convenience and out-of-season options. Generic brands are generally fine; just be sure to look at the ingredient label to check for any additives.

Minimally Processed Foods

Minimally processed plant-based foods are processed to some degree but have not been highly refined. For example, canned beans have been cooked so you can pop open a can, drain and rinse the beans, and enjoy them straight out of the can. Whole-grain pastas, tortillas, and some breads, as well as tofu and various unsweetened plant-based milks, fall into this category.

I consider foods with no more than two ingredients in the package to be more on par with a whole food than minimally processed. Others, such as grains

Always, Sometimes, Never

Here are a few examples of the "always" foods that make up the base of the WFPB diet, the "sometimes" foods that are best enjoyed in moderation, and the "never" foods that aren't part of the diet at all. Note that WFPB and WFPBSOS-free diets are slightly different, and those differences are accounted for here.

ALWAYS	SOMETIMES	NEVER
Whole foods eaten as close to their natural state as possible; no animal products	Plant-based foods higher in fat or sugar minimally processed plant-based foods; salt, oils, sugars (if not SOS-free)	Animal products; highly processed foods; salt, oils, and sugars (if SOS-free)
Whole grains: rice, oats, barley, quinoa, corn	**High-fat plant foods:** nuts, seeds, avocados	**Meat:** beef, pork, chicken, lamb, venison, buffalo
Fruits: apples, bananas, citrus, berries, melons, stone fruit	**Lightly processed foods:** whole-grain bread, whole-grain pasta, tofu	**Seafood:** fish, shellfish, mollusks
Vegetables: leafy greens (kale, lettuce, spinach, arugula, chard), broccoli, cauliflower, tomatoes, peppers, celery, green beans	**Unsweetened plant-based milks:** soy milk, coconut milk, almond milk, cashew milk, macadamia milk, oat milk, hemp milk, rice milk	**Dairy:** milk, butter, ghee, cheese, ice cream, whey **Eggs** **If SOS-free:**
Starchy vegetables: potatoes, sweet potatoes, carrots, beets	**Sweeteners:** maple syrup, date paste, date syrup, molasses	**Added salt** **All oils:** olive oil, sesame oil, canola oil, palm oil, peanut oil, coconut oil
Legumes: beans, peas, lentils		**Added sugar**
Mushrooms		**Processed vegan foods:** processed meat alternatives, packaged snacks, vegan ice cream
Aromatics: herbs and spices, onion, garlic, ginger, turmeric		

that have been milled into flour and then processed to become pasta, bread, or tortillas, should make up a small percentage of your overall plant-based diet. Think of them as occasional side dishes rather than a daily item or main course. And if you're trying to lose weight, consider skipping them completely in favor of the whole food itself (for example, eating a bowl of lentils instead of a bowl of lentil pasta).

A special note about tofu and the concern over hormones: Occasionally eating tofu can be fine for your diet. According to "Straight Talk About Soy," an article from Harvard University's School of Public Health, soy is a good source of protein that is safe to eat several times a week.

Fundamentals of Plant-Based Cooking

Plant-based home cooking is fundamentally different from what's known as the standard American diet because of the obvious absence of any animal-based products, including meat, dairy, and eggs. Even for those not completely eschewing salt, oil, and sugar, these ingredients are often replaced by healthier whole food alternatives whenever it makes sense to do so.

But if we're not using butter, olive oil, bacon, sugar, or cheese, for example, how is it possible to develop rich, delicious depths of flavor and texture? It's simple, really. We use a variety of plant foods, herbs, spices, and condiments, prepared in ways you may not have considered before, to yield delicious results. We sweeten with dried fruit or maple syrup, use lemon juice or various vinegars to add acidity, and make creamy sauces with blended nuts or beans and nutritional yeast. For instance, whenever I make Scalloped Potatoes (page 39), they are every bit as creamy, comforting, and tasty as any other recipe laden with dairy products. The more your taste buds become accustomed to the flavors of whole foods, the more you will crave and enjoy them.

In this book, we will be sautéing, steaming, and cooking in your Instant Pot. Prior to eating a plant-based diet, I was dubious about sautéing without oil. Yet all vegetables have their own liquid locked inside their cells, and when exposed to heat, that liquid is released. Sometimes you don't need to add anything to the pan to sauté a vegetable—known as the dry sautéing method. If veggies start to stick, which could happen in the base of the stainless-steel Instant Pot inner pot, you can add a tablespoon or so of water or broth to release the veggies.

Tips for Cutting Out SOS from Your Diet

Salt can be tricky because sodium is a naturally occurring mineral that our bodies need to function normally. However, consuming too much sodium can contribute to developing chronic diseases. Unfortunately, anyone eating a diet of highly processed foods (of any kind—whether animal-based or derived from plants) is consuming an excess of sodium added during the manufacturing process. Look for canned vegetables and beans labeled as "no salt added." If you choose to use salt in your dishes, add it to taste by sprinkling it on lightly when serving.

One of the biggest challenges for people new to this type of plant-based eating is eliminating salt, oil, and sugar. This diet has caused controversy because we have been led to believe there are healthy oils such as olive oil, flaxseed oil, and coconut oil. But apparently that is not so when it comes to the endothelium, which is the lining of the heart and blood vessels. Even extra-virgin olive oil impairs your arteries' ability to relax and dilate normally, which is clearly bad for your heart. Another downside to oils of any kind is the empty calories. Oil contains more calories per gram than any other food.

All that aside, the easiest arguments against oil are that it simply is not a whole food, is highly refined, and is the opposite of nutrient dense. Instead of adding oil to your meals, you can eat your healthy fats in the form of nuts, seeds, avocados, and, yes, olives.

Refined sugars like white table sugar, although often derived from beets, are similar to oils: Any nutrients that the original food contained are stripped away in the refining process. Natural sweetness can be added using whole food alternatives, including dried fruits such as dates (date syrup is simply dates and water), plain unsweetened applesauce, or 100 percent pure maple syrup.

Why the Instant Pot Is Perfect for Plant-Based Cooking

Given that many meals for plant-based eaters include either beans or grains (or both!), which can require longer cooking times using traditional stovetop cooking, the Instant Pot can feel like a lifesaver because it saves so much time. One friend purchased an Instant Pot to use just as a rice cooker because it prepares grains so beautifully. You also don't have to plan ahead and soak beans overnight—most days I'm not that organized! With the Instant Pot, you simply pull out a bag of dried beans, add some veggies and liquid, and in about an hour, you can have a complete meal.

The settings on the Instant Pot seem like they were designed for our kind of healthy cooking. Steaming, sautéing, and pressure-cooking can all be done in the same pot quickly, with no fuss. You'll see a few potato recipes, like my Sweet Potato Hash with Swiss Chard (page 27) and Garlic-Herb Baby Potatoes (page 42), that start with pressure-cooking the potatoes. This process is so quick and gives potatoes a fabulous texture to build the rest of the dish around. I also love how rapidly and easily you can go from sautéing some aromatics to flipping a switch and pressure-cooking all in the same pot.

But don't think the Instant Pot is good for only hardier foods like beans, legumes, grains, and potatoes. You can make delicious vegetables of any kind using your Instant Pot. My family loves my Gingered Collard Greens (page 34), made very easily and quickly in the Instant Pot. You can even make soups, stews, chilis, and other entrées by simply tossing some ingredients into your Instant Pot and setting it; you'll have a meal ready, often in less than 30 minutes, perfect for weeknights and busy families.

Getting to Know the Pot

One reason some people get an Instant Pot and then put it in the back of a closet is because it can seem intimidating at first with all the buttons and settings. You can become more comfortable with your Instant Pot by simply following the recipes in this book. Before long, you'll feel like an Instant Pot pro!

Parts

The Instant Pot contains parts that are different from most appliances, but if you've ever used a traditional pressure cooker, you may be familiar with some of them already. Here is a list of the parts of your Instant Pot and their basic functions:

Cooker base: This includes the heating element that the cord plugs into, the pot handles, and the control panel on the front of the unit.

Inner pot: This is the stainless-steel pot where you place your ingredients. It is removable and dishwasher-safe.

Cover: This includes the steam release handle, the steam release mechanism, and the float valve on the top, in addition to the cover handle and small tabs that allow the lid to be placed into the handles on the sides of the unit. Turn it over, and on the inside you'll find the silicone sealing ring gasket, silicone cap for the float valve, anti-block shield, and a lid-locking pin.

Steam release handle: The knob on top of the lid can be adjusted to Venting or Sealing before cooking.

Float valve: Located on the cover, this element rises to seal the pot when it comes to pressure and drops after the pressure is released.

Control panel: This is where you tell the Instant Pot how to make the magic happen. Each model is slightly different, but they all include a digital display, function keys with indicators showing when that function is in use (such as Keep Warm or Pressure Cook), and buttons to adjust from low to high pressure.

Controls

The control panel is where you'll find all the buttons to operate the Instant Pot. Here is a tour of what you'll see, but keep in mind you need only a few main functions for the recipes in this book: Pressure Cook/Manual, Sauté, Keep Warm, and Cancel. Some models include a Start button as well.

LED digital display: This shows you where the Instant Pot is in the cooking process. When you begin to pressure-cook, it displays "on" until the pot comes to pressure and then will display the time remaining to cook. If the pot becomes too hot, it will say "hot," and it will read "off" when the unit is not cooking.

Cooking program buttons: Each model has different buttons and programs built in. On some models, you'll see Soup/Broth and Bean/Chili buttons, for example. In this book, however, I'm keeping it simple by using only the Pressure Cook, Sauté, and Steam functions. (The one exception is the Soy Yogurt on page 21, which uses the Yogurt button.)

Time adjust buttons: On the Instant Pot Duo, one of the most popular models, the time adjusts with a plus or minus button on the control panel. Other models feature a knob that turns left to right to adjust the time.

Pressure indicator: This is how much pressure is in the pot while cooking, either low or high. Most of the recipes in this book use high pressure when using the Pressure Cook function.

Other operation keys: Keep Warm, Delay Start, and Cancel are common functions on many Instant Pot models. Pressing Cancel will turn the pot to the off mode and stop whatever process is running.

Key Terminology

You'll notice there are some terms you need to know as you use your Instant Pot and prepare the recipes in this book.

Natural release: When the pressure-cooking time is completed, the pot will cool itself down, and the pressure will slowly decrease. The float valve will drop when the pressure has fully released and you can safely open the lid. This process can take up to 20 minutes or more, depending on how full your pot is.

Quick release: When the pressure-cooking time is completed, you can release the pressure quickly by turning the steam release handle to Venting. I recommend using a long-handled wooden spoon to turn the valve and placing a kitchen towel lightly over the steam release to protect yourself from the burning-hot steam.

Pot-in-pot cooking: Within the Instant Pot, there is a removable inner pot where you place your ingredients; it sits over the heating element inside the exterior pot with the control panel on the front. Sometimes you'll use an additional pot or cooking vessel placed inside the inner pot. Examples include when you make Peanut Butter and Jelly Oatmeal (page 24) or Lemon Cheezecake (page 104). You simply place a pot (or other heatproof bowl or pan) inside the Instant Pot, usually with some water, to cook the dish.

Using Your Instant Pot Safely

The Instant Pot is a new breed of pressure cooker and has made pressure-cooking safer than it's ever been. Yet, like with all appliances and cooking methods, there are a few things to keep in mind for safety:

- **Do not overfill the pot.** On the stainless-steel inner pot, there is a clear indicator that reads "PC Max ⅔," meaning when pressure-cooking, do not fill the pot past that line, which indicates two-thirds of the way full.

- **Be sure all parts are in working order and placed properly.** On the lid, the sealing handle, silicone ring, and float valve are critical safety elements. Do a quick double-check before setting the pot.

- **Place the pot on a heat-safe flat surface.** Although the exterior of the pot does not get burning hot, it's still safer to place it on a heat-resistant surface. Never place the pot on the stovetop to cook.

- **Keep the pot in one place.** After you have set the pot to cook, do not attempt to move it to a different location. You're dealing with boiling-hot steam and food under pressure, so let it be and allow the pot to work its magic hands-off.

- **Leave the lid in place until the float valve drops.** The purpose of the float valve is to indicate whether the amount of pressure in the pot is low or high; if the valve is up, the pressure is high, and it is dangerous to attempt to remove the lid.

- **Stay away from the steam.** Keep your hands, fingers, and face away when releasing the pressure, because the steam is released forcefully and can cause burns.

How to Use the Instant Pot

Although using an Instant Pot for the first time may feel intimidating with all the various buttons and controls, the process really is straightforward.

First, determine the recipe you'll make and gather your ingredients. If you're only pressure-cooking, you'll add the ingredients to the pot, keeping in mind not to overfill the pot beyond the "max fill" line. Then secure the lid, which can take a bit of practice if you've never done it. When the lid is on securely, the pot will make a series of beeps, which sounds like a little song.

After securing the lid, set the cooking function, time, and amount of pressure, as indicated in the recipe. Then, after a few seconds, the pot will beep and the LED indicator will read "on." When it comes to temperature, the screen will begin counting down the time you programmed.

When you are cooking with your Instant Pot, keep in mind that the total cooking time includes the time it takes for the pot to come to pressure (5 to 15 minutes), the pressure-cooking time, and the time for either a quick release (30 to 60 seconds) or natural release of pressure (anywhere from 5 to 20 minutes).

Adjusting Recipes for High-Altitude Cooking

Water evaporates faster at higher altitudes, so if you live in the mountains or anywhere more than 2,000 feet above sea level, you'll need to adjust your Instant Pot cooking times accordingly. Generally, you'll need to add 5 percent of cooking time for every 1,000 feet more than 2,000 feet above sea level.

For example, if my brother-in-law and his wife in Colorado Springs, who live at 6,035 feet, want to make my Apple and Cinnamon Steel-Cut Oatmeal (page 20), they'll have to increase the time by 20 percent and set the pot to cook on high pressure for 12 minutes (10 minutes × 20% = 2; 10 + 2 = 12).

After you've prepared and enjoyed your meal, it's time to clean the appliance. The stainless-steel inner pot is dishwasher-safe, but I find it's just as easy to give it a good cleaning by hand with a soapy sponge right after cooking. Parts of the lid can also be gently removed and cleaned, including the silicone ring inside the pot.

Stocking Your Plant-Based Kitchen

When I first began testing recipes for this cookbook, I didn't need to go to the grocery store for almost two weeks! That's because I keep my fridge and pantry well stocked with all the essential ingredients and tools for plant-based cooking. After you stock your own kitchen, you'll find it very easy to make almost anything from this cookbook without a special trip to the store.

Fridge Staples

These common, store-bought fresh ingredients will serve as the backbone for many of the recipes in this book.

Apples: Fresh apples can keep for several months in the refrigerator. I often use them to make applesauce, which is perfect for replacing oil, sweetening dishes, or simply eating as a snack.

Avocados: I like to use mashed avocados with a bit of lime juice and green onions to add a layer of fat and creaminess to a baked potato or as a topping for soups, stews, and Mexican-inspired dishes.

Carrots, celery, and peppers: This veggie trio, along with onions and garlic, acts as the base of many recipes and also makes a great snack served with a dip.

Leafy greens: Collard greens, kale, bok choy, cabbages, Swiss chard, lettuces, parsley, cilantro, and spinach are some of my go-to favorites. To save time, look for bagged cleaned greens (and sometimes even chopped) in the produce and freezer sections.

Lemons and limes: These citruses add great freshness, acidity, and a pop of flavor to so many dishes.

Mushrooms: There are multiple varieties available, and they can all add a meaty texture with an earthy, rustic flavor to your dishes.

Plant-based milk: You can either make your own or purchase any type of unsweetened plant-based milk you prefer, including rice milk, oat milk, soy milk, hemp milk, coconut milk, and almond, cashew, or macadamia nut milks.

Tofu: I always keep all three types of tofu—silken, firm, and extra firm—on hand to make dips and sauces or to cut into chunks or crumbles.

White miso paste: Made from soybeans or chickpeas, white miso paste adds a salty, complex umami flavor to sauces and dishes. You can usually find it in the produce section, the refrigerated health-food section, or the Asian foods aisle. Chickpea miso paste is a soy-free alternative made from brown rice koji and chickpeas.

Pantry Staples

The recipes in this book lean heavily on these pantry staples to allow you to make a meal anytime.

Beans and lentils: Canned or dried, these legumes are high in fiber and are excellent sources of protein. Be sure to rinse dried legumes well before using, and sort through them to find and discard any debris.

Canned coconut milk: Full fat, low fat, and coconut cream are all used to add richness and depth to the recipes in this book.

Canned tomatoes: No-salt-added tomatoes—diced, crushed, sauce, and paste—can serve as the base for any number of soups, stews, chilis, and curries.

Dates and raisins: Versatile natural sweeteners and easy snacks, dates and raisins are great to have on hand.

Grains: Brown rice, black rice, wild rice, farro, quinoa, bulgur, buckwheat, wheat berries, oats, and cornmeal are all easy to find and cook up perfectly in the Instant Pot.

Nutritional yeast: Not at all the same as the typical yeast for baking, this yellow flaky powder adds a nutty, cheesy flavor and helps create amazing creamy sauces.

Nuts: Cashews, walnuts, almonds, peanuts, peanut butter, and pecans can be transformed into amazing dishes, like Lentil-Walnut Pâté (page 38).

Onions and garlic: These aromatics are flavor enhancers and create the base of every soup, stew, and chili in this cookbook.

Potatoes: Sweet potatoes, yellow or Yukon Gold potatoes, red potatoes, and russet potatoes can become breakfast, lunch, or dinner with ease.

Equipment Essentials

Although the Instant Pot works perfectly on its own with just the parts it comes with, you'll find that investing in a few accessories is well worth the additional expense by saving you time and allowing you the greatest flexibility with your recipes.

7-inch-round springform pan: Many springform pans on the market are 9 or 10 inches, so look for a smaller one that will fit inside your Instant Pot to make "cheezecakes" and more.

7-inch-round, 3-inch-deep oven-safe ceramic bowl: I had one of these in my kitchen long before getting an Instant Pot, and I discovered that it fits perfectly for pot-in-pot cooking. (A 7-inch-round metal cake pan should also fit inside the Instant Pot.)

Extra silicone sealing ring: If you notice a funky smell in your Instant Pot, it's probably coming from this ring, which absorbs odors from the foods you cook. Some people like to have two on hand: one for savory foods and one for sweet foods.

Instant Pot tempered-glass lid: This allows you to use your Instant Pot as a slow cooker as well as a pressure cooker.

Mini loaf pans (set of two): In the most common Instant Pot sizes, you can fit two mini loaf pans side by side.

Silicone baking cups: With these reusable cups, you can make muffins and cupcakes in the Instant Pot.

Steamer basket: Whether you opt for a metal or silicone steamer basket, you'll reach for this time and again whenever you need to steam potatoes or veggies.

Troubleshooting

Part of the beauty of the Instant Pot is that it's easy to use, especially when you're following a recipe. But nothing is completely foolproof, and sometimes you may encounter an issue. Here are a few of the most common problems and how to address them:

Undercooked grains or legumes: This is often caused by cooking with too little liquid—try adding a bit more next time. Salting dried beans before they are softened can also prevent them from fully cooking. (I once made this mistake, and my navy beans still weren't fully softened after *three whole days* of cooking using the slow-cooker function on my Instant Pot!)

Excess liquid after cooking: After using the Pressure Cook function, you may find some excess liquid on top of the food. You have a few options: (1) Stir the food after removing the lid and allow the liquid to absorb into the food (this is sufficient for many recipes); (2) Turn on the Sauté function and allow the liquid to cook off; or (3) Carefully spoon off and discard the excess liquid.

Burn warning: This is a common issue with Instant Pots and arises because the pot is overheating or there is food stuck to the bottom that is burning. The problem is often a lack of true liquid, like water, broth, or even juice. Tomato sauces and plant-based milks will sometimes burn if not combined with another liquid. When you see a burn warning, cancel the cooking process, do a quick release of the pressure, remove the lid, and inspect the pot. If there is food stuck to the bottom, you will need to scrape it off and discard it. If there is not enough liquid, you may need to add ½ to 1 cup of water or broth. Finally, I find the easiest way to avoid a burn notice is to use the pot-in-pot method of cooking.

The Recipes in This Book

In this book, you'll find recipes written for people following a whole food, plant-based diet, though some dishes contain ingredients that are not SOS-free. To find recipes that are SOS-free, look for the whole food, plant-based (WFPB) label at the top of the page (although these recipes may include salt as an optional ingredient).

These recipes can be made with any size or model of the Instant Pot. I've also written each with your ease of use in mind, and you'll see a few labels to help you decide what recipe you'd like to make. You'll find one-pot meals, recipes that contain five or fewer ingredients (not including water, oil, salt, and pepper), quick recipes that can be made in a total of 30 minutes or less, and those that are "worth the wait" (or take 45 minutes or longer to prepare and cook). Most recipes are designed to yield four to six servings, perfect for a busy household or plenty for leftovers if you're cooking for only one or two.

I've also included labels to indicate which recipes are gluten-free, nut-free, and soy-free. If you're cooking for someone with an allergy, take a moment to double-check the labels of your ingredients to be sure they don't contain any harmful additives or possible allergens.

GLUTEN-FREE   NUT-FREE   SOY-FREE   WFPB   5 OR FEWER INGREDIENTS

ONE-POT MEAL   QUICK   WORTH THE WAIT

Nutty Maple Polenta, page 28

CHAPTER 2
Breakfasts

Apple and Cinnamon Steel-Cut Oatmeal

GLUTEN-FREE NUT-FREE SOY-FREE WFPB 5 OR FEWER INGREDIENTS
ONE-POT MEAL QUICK

PREP TIME: 5 minutes **COOK SETTING:** High Pressure for 10 minutes **RELEASE:** Natural for 10 minutes, then quick **TOTAL TIME:** 30 minutes

Oatmeal is a common breakfast on a whole food, plant-based diet for good reason: It's got loads of fiber, it's inexpensive, it's fast and easy to make, and it tastes delicious. For even more flavor, add a splash of plant-based milk, a few raisins, some ground flaxseed for extra fiber, and nuts for crunch. **Serves 4 to 6**

5 cups water

2 cups gluten-free steel-cut oats

1 apple, cored and diced

3 tablespoons maple syrup

1 teaspoon ground cinnamon

1. In your Instant Pot, stir together the water, oats, apple, maple syrup, and cinnamon. Lock the lid and turn the steam release handle to Sealing. Using the Pressure Cook/Manual function, set the cooker to High Pressure for 10 minutes.

2. When the cook time is complete, let the pressure release naturally for 10 minutes; quick-release any remaining pressure and carefully remove the lid. There will be some liquid on top of the oatmeal. Stir well to incorporate it and serve immediately.

3. Store in the fridge for up to 4 days in a covered container. The oatmeal will thicken in the fridge but will loosen up when you reheat it in the microwave or on the stovetop over medium heat.

VARIATION TIP: The apple in this recipe almost melts away into the oats as everything cooks. If you prefer the texture of raw apple, you can dice a second apple and stir it into the oatmeal just before serving.

PER SERVING: Calories: 404; Fat: 7g; Protein: 8g; Total Carbs: 79g; Fiber: 9g; Sugar: 16g; Sodium: 2mg

Soy Yogurt

GLUTEN-FREE **NUT-FREE** **WFPB** **5 OR FEWER INGREDIENTS** **WORTH THE WAIT**

PREP TIME: 1 minute **COOK SETTING:** Yogurt for 15 hours **RELEASE:** None
TOTAL TIME: 15 hours 5 minutes

The secret to perfectly creamy homemade dairy-free yogurt is to use shelf-stable soy milk with only two ingredients: soybeans and water. Any other ingredients will interfere with the cultures. Speaking of cultures, you can purchase pull-apart probiotic capsules and pour out enough to get to the 12 billion CFUs needed. *Serves 4 to 6*

1 (32-ounce) carton unsweetened plain soy milk (containing *only* soybeans and water)

12 billion CFU probiotics

VARIATION TIP: In place of the probiotic capsule(s), you can substitute ½ cup plain plant-based yogurt with active cultures. Whisk in the yogurt with your soy milk and proceed with the recipe.

1. Pour the soy milk into your Instant Pot. Open the probiotic capsule and empty the powder into the milk, discarding the capsule itself. Whisk well to combine. Lock the lid and turn the steam release handle to Venting to allow steam to gently escape during the fermentation process. Using the Yogurt function, set the cooker for 15 hours.

2. When the cook time is complete, carefully remove the lid. There may be some liquid on top of the yogurt. If your probiotics were light pink, you may also notice some residual color from the powder. Using a large spoon, carefully remove and discard any excess liquid, then transfer the yogurt to a container or several glass or plastic jars to chill in the fridge. The yogurt will thicken further as it cools. For thicker Greek-style yogurt, strain the yogurt through a clean muslin cloth for 15 to 20 minutes.

3. Save ½ cup of your yogurt as a starter for the next batch. The more times you make the yogurt, the better each batch will become.

PER SERVING: Calories: 75; Fat: 4g; Protein: 7g; Total Carbs: 4g; Fiber: 1g; Sugar: 1g; Sodium: 79mg

Banana Bread Mini Loaves

GLUTEN-FREE **NUT-FREE** **SOY-FREE** **WORTH THE WAIT**

PREP TIME: 15 minutes **COOK SETTING:** High Pressure for 50 minutes **RELEASE:** Natural for 10 minutes, then quick **TOTAL TIME:** 1 hour 30 minutes

Banana bread has long been a family favorite and one of the best ways to use up bananas that are past their peak. Here, we nestle together two mini loaf pans in the Instant Pot. **Serves 4 to 6**

1 tablespoon ground flaxseed

2½ tablespoons water, plus 1 cup

1¼ cups gluten-free oat flour

1½ teaspoons baking powder

½ teaspoon baking soda

½ teaspoon ground cinnamon

⅛ teaspoon salt

1 very ripe banana, peeled

⅓ cup maple syrup

3 tablespoons Simple Applesauce (page 114) or no-sugar-added store-bought

1 teaspoon pure vanilla extract

Nonstick cooking spray

INGREDIENT TIP: Use the ripest bananas for the best flavor.

1. In a small bowl, stir together the flaxseed and the 2½ tablespoons of water.

2. In a large bowl, whisk together the oat flour, baking powder, baking soda, cinnamon, and salt. Spray 2 mini loaf pans with nonstick spray and set aside.

3. In a medium bowl, mash the banana, then whisk in the maple syrup, applesauce, vanilla, and flaxseed mixture. Pour into the dry ingredients and stir well.

4. Spray 2 mini loaf pans with nonstick cooking spray and divide the batter evenly between them. Cover with a few layers of paper towels and then wrap tightly with aluminum foil.

5. Pour the remaining 1 cup of water into your Instant Pot and insert the trivet. Place the loaf pans side by side on the trivet. Lock and seal the lid. Using the Pressure Cook/Manual function, set the cooker to High Pressure for 50 minutes.

6. When the cook time is complete, release the pressure naturally for 10 minutes; quick-release any remaining pressure and remove the lid. Remove the loaf pans, discard the foil and paper towel covers, and cool for 5 minutes before turning the breads out onto a cooling rack to cool for 10 more minutes before slicing.

PER SERVING: Calories: 245; Fat: 4g; Protein: 5g; Total Carbs: 49g; Fiber: 4g; Sugar: 21g; Sodium: 247mg

Breakfast Potatoes, Onions, and Peppers

GLUTEN-FREE **NUT-FREE** **SOY-FREE** **WFPB** **5 OR FEWER INGREDIENTS**
ONE-POT MEAL **QUICK**

PREP TIME: 10 minutes **COOK SETTING:** High Pressure for 5 minutes **RELEASE:** Natural for 5 minutes, then quick **TOTAL TIME:** 30 minutes

The first step to making this hearty breakfast dish is to steam the potatoes. If you don't have a steamer basket, you can cover the trivet with foil and poke some holes in it with the tines of a fork. Place the potatoes on top and *boom*—instant steamer! **Serves 4 to 6**

1 cup water

2 pounds red or yellow potatoes, cubed into 1½-inch chunks

1 medium onion, diced

1 bell pepper, diced

1 teaspoon garlic powder

¾ teaspoon paprika

Freshly ground black pepper

Salt (optional)

VARIATION TIP: If you prefer crispier potatoes, add 2 tablespoons of plant-based butter while sautéing.

1. Pour the water into your Instant Pot. Place the potatoes in a steamer basket inside the pot, or use the foil method described in the headnote. Lock the lid and turn the steam release handle to Sealing. Using the Pressure Cook/Manual function, set the cooker to High Pressure for 5 minutes.

2. When the cook time is complete, let the pressure release naturally for 5 minutes; quick-release any remaining pressure and carefully remove the lid. Remove the steamer basket and the potatoes and drain the inner pot.

3. Replace the inner pot and turn on the Sauté function. Allow the pot to preheat for 3 minutes, then combine the onion and pepper in the pot and sauté for about 3 minutes. If the veggies begin to stick, slowly add water, a tablespoon at a time. Add the potatoes, garlic powder, paprika, black pepper, and salt (if using) and cook until the vegetables are done to your liking. Serve immediately.

PER SERVING: Calories: 179; Fat: 0g; Protein: 5g; Total Carbs: 41g; Fiber: 5g; Sugar: 5g; Sodium: 44mg

Peanut Butter and Jelly Oatmeal

PREP TIME: 3 minutes   **COOK SETTING:** High Pressure for 3 minutes   **RELEASE:** Natural for 10 minutes, then quick   **TOTAL TIME:** 25 minutes

For creamier oatmeal with less chew than steel-cut oats, I like to cook old-fashioned oats in my Instant Pot using the pot-in-pot method. This recipe is completely hands-off and, unlike the stovetop method, you won't have to worry about the oatmeal boiling over and making a mess! *Serves 4 to 6*

2 cups gluten-free old-fashioned rolled oats

2 cups unsweetened plant-based milk

1 tablespoon ground flaxseed

3 cups water, divided

½ cup peanut butter

½ cup Strawberry Compote (page 115) or no-sugar-added fruit preserves

1. In a heatproof bowl, stir together the oats, milk, flaxseed, and 2 cups of the water. Place the trivet in your Instant Pot and pour in the remaining 1 cup of water. Place the bowl with the oatmeal mixture on top of the trivet. Lock the lid and turn the steam release handle to Sealing. Using the Pressure Cook/Manual function, set the cooker to High Pressure for 3 minutes.

2. When the cook time is complete, let the pressure release naturally for 10 minutes; quick-release any remaining pressure and carefully remove the lid. There may be some liquid on top of the oatmeal. Add the peanut butter and stir well to incorporate. Top each serving with about 2 tablespoons of the compote and serve immediately.

3. Store in the fridge for up to 4 days in a covered container.

FLAVOR BOOST: Add fresh fruit and nuts for extra texture and flavor. I love topping my oatmeal with banana slices and whole peanuts.

PER SERVING: Calories: 405; Fat: 22g; Protein: 17g; Total Carbs: 39g; Fiber: 7g; Sugar: 6g; Sodium: 51mg

Spinach-Mushroom Tofu Scramble

GLUTEN-FREE   NUT-FREE   WFPB   ONE-POT MEAL   QUICK

PREP TIME: 5 minutes   **COOK SETTING:** Sauté for 10 to 12 minutes   **RELEASE:** None
Total time: 17 minutes

When you're craving a quick, savory breakfast, this tofu scramble is a satisfying and healthy choice. Here I use spinach and mushrooms, but you can swap in whatever combination of veggies you love best, such as chopped zucchini, bell pepper, chard, or asparagus. **Serves 4 to 6**

1 medium onion, diced

1 medium red bell pepper, diced

2 tablespoons no-salt-added veggie broth or water, divided

1 garlic clove, minced

1 (14-ounce) package firm tofu, drained and crumbled

2 teaspoons ground turmeric

½ teaspoon garlic powder

½ teaspoon paprika

3 ounces fresh baby spinach

Salt (optional)

Freshly ground black pepper

1. Select the Sauté function on your Instant Pot and allow it to preheat for 3 minutes. Combine the onion and bell pepper in the pot with 1 tablespoon of the broth and sauté until the onion begins to brown and the bell pepper is soft, about 5 minutes, adding a teaspoon more of broth at a time to keep the veggies from sticking. Stir in the minced garlic.

2. Add the tofu, turmeric, garlic powder, and paprika. Stir to combine and cook until the tofu has a yellowish color that resembles scrambled eggs.

3. Add the spinach and stir. Cook about 5 more minutes, until the tofu is heated through and the spinach is just wilted. Season to taste with salt (if using) and black pepper. Serve immediately.

INGREDIENT TIP: There are three styles of tofu: silken, firm, and extra firm. Firm or extra firm works well with this recipe, but be sure to drain either thoroughly before using. However, there's no need to press it for this recipe; the remaining liquid in the tofu blends with the veggies and spices to create a nice finished texture.

PER SERVING: Calories: 103; Fat: 4g; Protein: 10g; Total Carbs: 9g; Fiber: 3g; Sugar: 3g; Sodium: 32mg

Triple-Berry Breakfast Quinoa

GLUTEN-FREE **WFPB** **ONE-POT MEAL** **QUICK**

PREP TIME: 3 minutes **COOK SETTING:** High Pressure for 2 minutes **RELEASE:** Natural for 5 minutes, then quick **TOTAL TIME:** 25 minutes

Oats aren't the only grain that belong on your breakfast table. Nutty quinoa cooks up beautifully in this recipe with plant-based milk and frozen berries. The result is a delicious, colorful breakfast that couldn't be easier to whip up. **Serves 4 to 6**

1 cup white quinoa, rinsed

1¾ cups unsweetened plant-based milk

½ cup frozen blueberries

½ cup frozen strawberries

½ cup frozen raspberries

¼ cup maple syrup

2 teaspoons pure vanilla extract

1 cup water

1. In a heatproof bowl, stir together the quinoa, milk, blueberries, strawberries, raspberries, maple syrup, and vanilla. Place the trivet inside your Instant Pot and pour in the water. Place the bowl with the quinoa mixture on top of the trivet. Lock the lid and turn the steam release handle to Sealing. Using the Pressure Cook/Manual function, set the cooker to High Pressure for 2 minutes.

2. When the cook time is complete, let the pressure release naturally for 5 minutes; quick-release any remaining pressure and carefully remove the lid. Stir well to combine, then serve immediately.

3. Store in the fridge for up to 4 days in a covered container. Reheat in the microwave, adding a bit more milk, as the quinoa will thicken in the fridge.

INGREDIENT TIP: Be sure to use white quinoa rather than red or black quinoa, which takes longer to cook. And unless the package says the quinoa is prerinsed, don't skip that step. Washing breaks the bitter outer membrane from the grain and will yield a much better finished flavor.

PER SERVING: Calories: 277; Fat: 5g; Protein: 9g; Total Carbs: 49g; Fiber: 6g; Sugar: 16g; Sodium: 43mg

Sweet Potato Hash with Swiss Chard

GLUTEN-FREE **WFPB** **ONE-POT MEAL** **QUICK**

PREP TIME: 10 minutes **COOK SETTING:** High Pressure for 6 minutes, Sauté for 7 to 10 minutes **RELEASE:** Quick **TOTAL TIME:** 30 minutes

I once had some beautiful rainbow Swiss chard on hand and added it to my favorite hash—and I loved it! Swiss chard has a mild, sweet taste and brings one more layer of flavor to this savory breakfast. **Serves 4 to 6**

1 cup water

4 medium sweet potatoes, peeled and diced

1 medium red onion, diced

1 medium red or green bell pepper, diced

1 teaspoon garlic powder

1 teaspoon smoked paprika

Freshly ground black pepper

Salt (optional)

4 to 6 leaves Swiss chard, woody stems removed and discarded, greens chopped

¼ cup unsweetened plant-based milk

1. Pour the water into your Instant Pot. Place the sweet potatoes in a steamer basket inside the pot. Lock the lid and turn the steam release handle to Sealing. Using the Pressure Cook/Manual function, set the cooker to High Pressure for 6 minutes.

2. When the cook time is complete, quick-release the pressure and carefully remove the lid. Remove the steamer basket and sweet potatoes and drain the inner pot.

3. Replace the inner pot and select the Sauté function. Sauté the onion and bell pepper for 3 to 5 minutes, adding water as needed to prevent sticking. Add the sweet potatoes, garlic powder, paprika, black pepper, and salt (if using) and cook for another 1 to 2 minutes. Add the Swiss chard and sauté until wilted, about 3 more minutes. Add the milk, scraping the bottom of the pot as you stir, then serve immediately.

INGREDIENT TIP: Feel free to substitute a couple of shallots or a yellow or white onion for the red onion.

PER SERVING: Calories: 154; Fat: 1g; Protein: 4g; Total Carbs: 34g; Fiber: 6g; Sugar: 9g; Sodium: 210mg

Nutty Maple Polenta

GLUTEN-FREE   WFPB   5 OR FEWER INGREDIENTS   ONE-POT MEAL   QUICK

PREP TIME: 2 minutes   **COOK SETTING:** Sauté for 5 minutes, High Pressure for 10 minutes   **RELEASE:** Quick   **TOTAL TIME:** 20 minutes

This porridge is made from coarsely ground cornmeal (known alternatively as polenta or grits). For another way of serving polenta, pour the cooked dish into a loaf pan and let it set for a few hours until firm before cutting it. Reheat slices in the microwave for 30 to 60 seconds and top with more maple syrup and a handful of your favorite berries. **Serves 4 to 6**

3 cups water

2 cups unsweetened plant-based milk

1 cup polenta

½ cup pecan or walnut pieces

¼ cup maple syrup

1. Select the Sauté function on your Instant Pot and whisk together the water, milk, and polenta in the pot. Continue to whisk frequently for 5 minutes, until the mixture reaches a simmer, then cancel the Sauté function. Lock the lid and turn the steam release handle to Sealing. Using the Pressure Cook/Manual function, set the cooker to High Pressure for 10 minutes.

2. When the cook time is complete, quick-release the pressure and carefully remove the lid. Add the nuts and maple syrup and stir well to combine. Serve immediately.

3. Store in the fridge for up to 4 days in a covered container. The polenta will thicken in the fridge but will loosen up when you reheat it in the microwave or on the stovetop over medium heat.

VARIATION TIP: Turn this into a savory breakfast by omitting the maple syrup and nuts and adding sautéed fresh veggies like mushrooms, zucchini, spinach, chard, or kale. Top with fresh tomatoes or salsa and sprinkle with a bit of plant-based parmesan cheese.

PER SERVING: Calories: 319; Fat: 12g; Protein: 9g; Total Carbs: 45g; Fiber: 4g; Sugar: 15g; Sodium: 327mg

Blueberry Muffins

GLUTEN-FREE **QUICK**

PREP TIME: 10 minutes **COOK SETTING:** High Pressure for 9 minutes
RELEASE: Quick **TOTAL TIME:** 30 minutes

These blueberry muffins are perfectly moist from being cooked in the Instant Pot. Because they are essentially steamed, the color will be consistent throughout; don't expect them to get brown on top. Also, be sure to remove the lid immediately after cooking to avoid water dripping on top of them. **Makes 6 muffins**

1 cup gluten-free flour blend (substitute white whole wheat flour if not gluten-free)

¼ cup gluten-free old-fashioned rolled oats

2 teaspoons baking powder

Pinch of salt

¼ cup maple syrup

¼ cup Simple Applesauce (page 114) or no-sugar-added store-bought

2 tablespoons unsweetened plant-based milk

1 tablespoon chia seeds

1 teaspoon pure vanilla extract

½ cup blueberries

1 cup water

1. In a medium bowl, whisk together the flour, oats, baking powder, and salt. Set aside.

2. In a small bowl, whisk together the maple syrup, applesauce, milk, chia seeds, and vanilla. Pour over the dry ingredients and stir until just moistened. Fold in the blueberries. Evenly divide the batter among 6 silicone baking cups.

3. Pour the water into your Instant Pot and place the trivet inside. Carefully place each baking cup on top of the trivet. Lock the lid and turn the steam release handle to Sealing. Using the Pressure Cook/Manual function, set the cooker to High Pressure for 9 minutes.

4. When the cook time is complete, quick-release the pressure and carefully remove the lid. Remove the muffins to a cooling rack to cool for at least 10 minutes before serving.

VARIATION TIP: Lemon and blueberry is a classic flavor combination. Add the zest of 1 lemon and 1 tablespoon of lemon juice, and reduce the milk to 1 tablespoon for Lemon Blueberry Muffins.

PER SERVING: Calories: 149; Fat: 1g; Protein: 3g; Total Carbs: 32g; Fiber: 2g; Sugar: 10g; Sodium: 30mg

Scalloped Potatoes, page 39

CHAPTER 3
Sides and Appetizers

Cauliflower Queso

GLUTEN-FREE **WFPB** **QUICK**

PREP TIME: 5 minutes **COOK SETTING:** High Pressure for 5 minutes **RELEASE:** Quick
TOTAL TIME: 25 minutes

My dad's favorite day of the year was Super Bowl Sunday, and we could always count on a warm bowl of creamy queso to enjoy with the big game. This version is just as delicious, but 100 percent WFPB compliant. Serve it with your favorite tortilla chips, raw veggies, or baked potato wedges for dipping. **Makes about 5 cups**

1 head cauliflower, cut into about 4 cups florets

2 cups water

1½ cups carrots, chopped into ½-inch-thick round pieces

½ cup raw cashews

1 (15-ounce) can no-salt-added diced tomatoes, divided

½ cup nutritional yeast

1 tablespoon white miso paste

2 teaspoons gluten-free chili powder

1 red bell pepper, diced

4 scallions, white and green parts, diced

1. In your Instant Pot, combine the cauliflower, water, carrots, and cashews. Lock the lid and turn the steam release handle to Sealing. Using the Pressure Cook/Manual function, set the cooker to High Pressure for 5 minutes.

2. When the cook time is complete, quick-release the pressure and carefully remove the lid.

3. Drain the water, then transfer the mixture to a blender or food processor. Add the liquid from the can of tomatoes and set the drained tomatoes aside. Add the nutritional yeast, miso, and chili powder and blend until very smooth. Transfer to a medium bowl and stir in the drained tomatoes, bell pepper, and scallions. Serve immediately. Store any leftovers in the fridge for up to 4 days in a covered container.

LEFTOVER TIP: Use leftover dip as a topping for baked potatoes, stirred into mashed potatoes, or mixed into cooked brown rice for a satisfying side dish. You can also thin it with a bit of plant-based milk, heat it, and serve it as a Southwestern-style cheeze soup.

PER SERVING (½ CUP): Calories: 77; Fat: 4g; Protein: 3g; Total Carbs: 10g; Fiber: 3g; Sugar: 4g; Sodium: 114mg

Baba Ghanoush

GLUTEN-FREE NUT-FREE WFPB QUICK

PREP TIME: 5 minutes **COOK SETTING:** Sauté for 8 minutes, High Pressure for 3 minutes
RELEASE: Quick **TOTAL TIME:** 25 minutes

I tasted this garlicky eggplant dip for the first time while I was living in Paris, at the home of some friends from Beirut. Although it's traditionally served cold, you could also eat it warm with raw veggies for dipping. **Makes about 2 cups**

¼ to ½ cup Easy Vegetable Broth (page 108) or no-salt-added vegetable broth, divided

1 medium eggplant, peeled and sliced into 1-inch-thick rounds

1 cup water

3 garlic cloves, unpeeled

2 tablespoons freshly squeezed lemon juice

2 tablespoons tahini

1 tablespoon white miso paste

½ teaspoon ground cumin, plus more for garnish

INGREDIENT TIP: You can find premade tahini in the grocery store, but be sure to check the ingredient label for additives. Good tahini should have only one ingredient: sesame seeds.

1. Select the Sauté function on your Instant Pot and pour in 2 tablespoons of the broth. Arrange as many slices of eggplant as possible in one layer on the bottom of the pot. Sauté for 2 minutes, then flip, adding more of the broth as needed. After another 2 minutes, pile the first batch of eggplant on one side of the Instant Pot and add the remaining eggplant. Sauté on each side for 2 minutes, adding broth as needed.

2. Add the water and garlic, then lock the lid and set the steam valve to Sealing. Using the Pressure Cook/Manual function, set the cooker to High Pressure for 3 minutes. When the cook time is complete, quick-release the pressure and carefully remove the lid.

3. Using a pair of tongs, remove the garlic and take off the outer peel. In a blender, combine the garlic, eggplant, lemon juice, tahini, miso, and cumin. Blend until smooth. Serve warm or cover, refrigerate, and serve cold. Store any leftovers in the fridge for up to 4 days in a covered container.

PER SERVING (⅓ CUP): Calories: 62; Fat: 3g; Protein: 2g; Total Carbs: 8g; Fiber: 3g; Sugar: 4g; Sodium: 110mg

Gingered Collard Greens

GLUTEN-FREE NUT-FREE SOY-FREE WFPB 5 OR FEWER INGREDIENTS QUICK

PREP TIME: 10 minutes **COOK SETTING:** High Pressure for 10 minutes **RELEASE:** Quick
TOTAL TIME: 25 minutes

I owe the idea for this recipe to the late Chef Rich, a friend who once owned a barbecue restaurant in Aurora, Illinois. His collard greens were some of the best I ever tasted. When he lived in Japan and ran a restaurant there, he began experimenting with a fusion of traditional American soul food and Japanese flavors. The secret ingredient to his collards—and now yours: fresh ginger. **Serves 4 to 6**

1½ pounds collard greens, stems removed, leaves chopped

1½ cups Easy Vegetable Broth (page 108) or no-salt-added vegetable broth

3 tablespoons rice vinegar

3 garlic cloves, minced

1 (2-inch) knob fresh ginger, grated

In your Instant Pot, combine the collard greens, broth, vinegar, garlic, and ginger. Lock the lid and set the steam valve to Sealing. Using the Pressure Cook/Manual function, set the cooker to High Pressure for 10 minutes. When the cook time is complete, quick-release the pressure and carefully remove the lid.

INGREDIENT TIP: Collard greens are sold in bundles of large leaves. You'll need to remove the woody stem and the vein it's attached to on each leaf before chopping. Alternatively, you can sometimes find fresh collard greens in the produce department that are prepackaged and chopped, with the stems and main vein already removed.

PER SERVING: Calories: 61; Fat: 1g; Protein: 5g; Total Carbs: 10g; Fiber: 7g; Sugar: 1g; Sodium: 30mg

Spiced Sweet Potatoes

GLUTEN-FREE **NUT-FREE** **SOY-FREE** **WFPB** **QUICK**

PREP TIME: 10 minutes **COOK SETTING:** High Pressure for 9 minutes **RELEASE:** Quick
TOTAL TIME: 25 minutes

The citrusy notes of orange juice marry perfectly with these sweet potatoes, and warm spices round out the dish and add complexity. While the potatoes cook, serve a salad of greens tossed with pears, walnuts, and apple cider vinaigrette and you'll have an easy weeknight meal ready in less than 30 minutes. *Serves 4 to 6*

- 4 or 5 medium sweet potatoes (about 2 pounds), peeled and cut into 1-inch chunks
- 1 cup freshly squeezed orange juice
- 2 garlic cloves, minced
- 1 (1-inch) knob fresh ginger, peeled and grated, or 1 teaspoon ground ginger
- 1 (1-inch) knob fresh turmeric, peeled and grated, or 1 teaspoon ground turmeric
- ½ teaspoon ground cinnamon
- 1 tablespoon maple syrup

1. In your Instant Pot, combine the sweet potatoes, orange juice, garlic, ginger, turmeric, and cinnamon. Lock the lid and turn the steam release handle to Sealing. Using the Pressure Cook/Manual function, set the cooker to High Pressure for 9 minutes.

2. When the cook time is complete, quick-release the pressure and carefully remove the lid. Add the maple syrup and mash the potatoes with a hand-held potato masher or a large fork. Stir to blend and serve immediately.

INGREDIENT TIP: Both ginger and turmeric are root vegetables known as rhizomes and contain antioxidants with anti-inflammatory properties. I like to buy them both fresh and store them in the freezer, where they will keep indefinitely.

PER SERVING: Calories: 243; Fat: 0g; Protein: 4g; Total Carbs: 57g; Fiber: 7g; Sugar: 18g; Sodium: 127mg

Brussels Sprouts with Sweet Dijon Vinaigrette

GLUTEN-FREE NUT-FREE SOY-FREE WFPB 5 OR FEWER INGREDIENTS QUICK

PREP TIME: 5 minutes **COOK SETTING:** High Pressure for 1 minute **RELEASE:** Quick
TOTAL TIME: 15 minutes

This recipe yields a creamy, dreamy, tangy side dish with just a touch of sweetness and is ready in only 15 minutes. As a bonus, you can use the dressing from this recipe on any salad or veggies. I often double or triple the dressing ingredients, combine them in a glass jar with a lid, and shake it well. It'll keep in the fridge for a couple of weeks. **Serves 4 to 6**

1 pound fresh
   Brussels sprouts

1 cup water

2 garlic cloves, smashed

3 tablespoons apple
   cider vinegar

2 tablespoons
   Dijon mustard

1 tablespoon maple syrup

Freshly ground
   black pepper

1. In your Instant Pot, combine the Brussels sprouts, water, and garlic. Lock the lid and turn the steam release handle to Sealing. Using the Pressure Cook/Manual function, set the cooker to High Pressure for 1 minute.

2. In a small bowl, whisk together the vinegar, mustard, and maple syrup. When the cook time is complete, quick-release the pressure and carefully remove the lid. Drain the water and mince the garlic. Add the dressing to the sprouts and garlic and toss to coat. Season with pepper and serve immediately.

VARIATION TIP: You can use frozen Brussels sprouts in this recipe without thawing them. If you do, increase the cook time to 2 minutes. If you prefer your Brussels sprouts crispy rather than creamy, remove the cooked sprouts after draining, select the Sauté function, add about 2 tablespoons of olive oil, and sauté the sprouts until they are golden brown.

PER SERVING: Calories: 71; Fat: 1g; Protein: 4g; Total Carbs: 15g; Fiber: 5g; Sugar: 6g; Sodium: 116mg

Jalapeño Popper Dip

GLUTEN-FREE **WFPB** **WORTH THE WAIT**

PREP TIME: 10 minutes **COOK SETTING:** High Pressure for 30 minutes **RELEASE:** Natural for 10 minutes, then quick **TOTAL TIME:** 1 hour

If you're a fan of spicy dips, you'll love this recipe. Be careful when chopping hot peppers: Use gloves or scrub your hands immediately after chopping so you don't accidentally burn your eyes. **Serves 4 to 6**

2 jalapeño peppers, divided

½ pound dried great northern beans, rinsed and sorted

½ medium onion, roughly chopped

4 cups water, divided

½ cup cashews

¼ cup unsweetened plant-based milk

2 garlic cloves, crushed

2 tablespoons nutritional yeast

1 tablespoon chickpea miso paste

1 tablespoon apple cider vinegar

LEFTOVERS TIP: Use leftover dip as a spicy spread for a tortilla stuffed with sautéed bell peppers, onions, and portobello mushrooms. Serve with a dollop of salsa or guacamole.

1. Slice 1 of the jalapeños in half lengthwise and remove the seeds. In your Instant Pot, combine the halved pepper, beans, onion, and 3 cups of the water. Lock the lid and turn the steam release handle to Sealing. Using the Pressure Cook/Manual function, set the cooker to High Pressure for 30 minutes.

2. Boil the remaining 1 cup of water and, using a large bowl, pour it over the cashews; let soak for at least 30 minutes. Drain and discard the soaking liquid before using the cashews.

3. When the cook time is complete, let the pressure release naturally for 10 minutes; quick-release any remaining pressure and carefully remove the lid. Remove the jalapeño from the pot and finely chop it. Finely chop the remaining raw jalapeño, removing the seeds if you prefer a milder dish. Set both peppers aside.

4. Drain the beans and onion, then combine them in a blender with the cashews, milk, garlic, nutritional yeast, miso, and vinegar. Blend until creamy. Spoon into a medium mixing bowl and stir in the jalapeños. Serve immediately. Store any leftovers in the fridge for up to 4 days in a covered container.

PER SERVING: Calories: 314; Fat: 9g; Protein: 17g; Total Carbs: 44g; Fiber: 13g; Sugar: 4g; Sodium: 177mg

Lentil-Walnut Pâté

GLUTEN-FREE **WFPB** **QUICK**

PREP TIME: 10 minutes **COOK SETTING:** Sauté for 3 to 5 minutes, High Pressure for 10 minutes **RELEASE:** Natural for 10 minutes, then quick **TOTAL TIME:** 30 minutes

While living in Paris, I fell in love with the delicious local dishes, some of which I'd never tasted before. One of my favorites was pâté spread on a piece of crusty French bread with a dab of mustard. This appetizer brings me right back to those days—yet it's even better than the original because it's made from plant-based foods. **Serves 4 to 6**

¾ cup walnuts

2 cups water

1 cup green or brown lentils

½ medium onion, roughly chopped

1 bay leaf

2 garlic cloves, minced

2 tablespoons freshly squeezed lemon juice

1 tablespoon white miso paste

1 tablespoon apple cider vinegar

Freshly ground black pepper

1. Select the Sauté function on your Instant Pot and allow it to preheat for 2 minutes. Pour in the walnuts and sauté for 3 to 5 minutes, stirring occasionally, until slightly darker in color and the oils begin to release. Remove from the Instant Pot and set aside.

2. In your Instant Pot, combine the water, lentils, onion, and bay leaf. Lock the lid and turn the steam release handle to Sealing. Using the Pressure Cook/Manual function, set the cooker to High Pressure for 10 minutes.

3. When the cook time is complete, let the pressure release naturally for 10 minutes; quick-release any remaining pressure and carefully remove the lid. Remove and discard the bay leaf. In a blender or food processor, combine the lentils, onion, garlic, lemon juice, miso, vinegar, and pepper to taste. Blend until creamy. Serve either immediately as a warm dip or chill.

INGREDIENT TIP: There are several types of lentils, but this pâté works best with either brown or green lentils.

PER SERVING (¼ CUP): Calories: 331; Fat: 15g; Protein: 16g; Total Carbs: 37g; Fiber: 7g; Sugar: 3g; Sodium: 163mg

Scalloped Potatoes

GLUTEN-FREE | WFPB | WORTH THE WAIT

PREP TIME: 15 minutes **COOK SETTING:** High Pressure for 27 minutes **RELEASE:** Quick
TOTAL TIME: 50 minutes

The key to this dish is slicing the potatoes *very* thinly so they cook thoroughly. If the potatoes are still too hard for your liking after cooking, cook for another 2 to 4 minutes in your Instant Pot. **Serves 4 to 6**

1 cup unsweetened plant-based milk

½ cup Easy Vegetable Broth (page 108) or no-salt-added vegetable broth

2 scallions, white and green parts, chopped

2 tablespoons nutritional yeast

1 tablespoon arrowroot powder

1 teaspoon garlic powder

1 teaspoon minced fresh rosemary

1 teaspoon mustard powder

Freshly ground black pepper

Salt (optional)

1½ pounds russet potatoes (4 or 5 medium), peeled

1 cup water

1. In a large mixing bowl, whisk together the milk, broth, scallions, nutritional yeast, arrowroot powder, garlic powder, rosemary, and mustard powder. Season to taste with pepper and salt (if using). Using a mandoline, the slicing blade on a food processor, or the slicing side of a box grater, slice the potatoes *very* thinly.

2. In a 7-inch-round ovenproof baking dish, arrange a 1-inch layer of potatoes, followed by enough of the sauce to just cover the potatoes. Continue layering until all the potatoes are submerged under the sauce in the dish.

3. Pour the water into your Instant Pot and insert the trivet. Place the dish on the trivet. Lock and seal the lid. Set the cooker to High Pressure for 27 minutes.

4. When the cook time is complete, quick-release the pressure and carefully remove the lid and the dish. Serve immediately.

FLAVOR BOOST: Create a crispy topping by melting 2 tablespoons of plant-based butter and stirring in 6 tablespoons of panko bread crumbs. Sprinkle over the potatoes before pressure-cooking. After pressure-cooking, place the dish under the broiler for 1 to 2 minutes, until golden brown.

PER SERVING: Calories: 172; Fat: 1g; Protein: 6g; Total Carbs: 36g; Fiber: 3g; Sugar: 3g; Sodium: 54mg

Mini Corn on the Cob with Tofu Crema

GLUTEN-FREE NUT-FREE WFPB QUICK

PREP TIME: 5 minutes **COOK SETTING:** High Pressure for 6 minutes **RELEASE:** Quick
TOTAL TIME: 15 minutes

This side dish is inspired by Mexican street corn, which is traditionally served on a stick. Crema, similar to sour cream but a bit thinner, is spread over the corn, then sprinkled with chili powder. Here, we make crema using tofu. **Serves 4 to 6**

1 cup water

4 to 6 frozen mini corncobs

1 (14-ounce) package silken tofu, drained

1 tablespoon freshly squeezed lemon juice

1 tablespoon apple cider vinegar

1 teaspoon ground cumin

Salt (optional)

1 lime, cut into wedges

1 tablespoon no-salt-added gluten-free chili powder

1. Pour the water into the Instant Pot and place the trivet inside. Set the corn on the trivet. Lock the lid and turn the steam release handle to Sealing. Set the cooker to High Pressure for 6 minutes.

2. In a blender or food processor, combine the tofu, lemon juice, vinegar, cumin, and salt to taste (if using). Blend well and set aside.

3. When the cook time is complete, quick-release the pressure and carefully remove the lid. Rub each cob with a lime wedge and then slather it with a generous amount of crema. Sprinkle ¼ to ½ teaspoon chili powder on each. Serve immediately. Store any leftovers in the fridge for up to 4 days in a covered container.

LEFTOVERS TIP: Use leftover crema in a slaw to top "fish" tacos made from hearts of palm. Drain and shred a 14-ounce can of hearts of palm, season with chili powder, and bake on a baking sheet at 425°F for 10 minutes. Combine 2 chopped scallions (white and green parts) with a 16-ounce bag of coleslaw mix and stir in about ½ cup of tofu crema. Serve the hearts of palm on warmed corn tortillas with the slaw and a dollop of guacamole.

PER SERVING: Calories: 103; Fat: 4g; Protein: 8g; Total Carbs: 12g; Fiber: 2g; Sugar: 2g; Sodium: 68mg

Beet Hummus

GLUTEN-FREE NUT-FREE SOY-FREE WFPB 5 OR FEWER INGREDIENTS WORTH THE WAIT

PREP TIME: 5 minutes **COOK SETTING:** High Pressure for 45 minutes **RELEASE:** Natural for 10 minutes, then quick **TOTAL TIME:** 1 hour 5 minutes

This simple dip is packed with complex flavors: earthiness from the beets, brightness from the lemon juice, creaminess from the tahini, and a bite from the garlic. The resulting deep pink or light red color (depending on the size of your beet) makes a beautiful addition to any appetizer table or side dish for falafel sandwiches. *Serves 4 to 6*

3 cups water

1 cup dried chickpeas, rinsed and sorted

1 medium beet, peeled and quartered

½ cup tahini

2 tablespoons freshly squeezed lemon juice

4 garlic cloves, crushed

Salt (optional)

1. In your Instant Pot, combine the water, chickpeas, and beets. Lock the lid and turn the steam release handle to Sealing. Using the Pressure Cook/Manual function, set the cooker to High Pressure for 45 minutes.

2. When the cook time is complete, let the pressure release naturally for 10 minutes; quick-release any remaining pressure and carefully remove the lid. In a blender or food processor, combine the tahini, lemon juice, garlic, and salt to taste (if using). Using a slotted spoon, remove the chickpeas and beets from the pot and add them to the other ingredients. Blend well to combine, adding a tablespoon at a time of the remaining liquid in the Instant Pot if necessary to thin the dip. Chill until cool.

VARIATION TIP: For a beautiful golden color, substitute golden beets for the red beets and add ½ teaspoon ground turmeric. If you're not a fan of beets, leave them out and make a more traditional hummus by adding 1 teaspoon ground cumin and ¼ teaspoon paprika.

PER SERVING: Calories: 382; Fat: 19g; Protein: 16g; Total Carbs: 41g; Fiber: 10g; Sugar: 7g; Sodium: 63mg

Garlic-Herb Baby Potatoes

GLUTEN-FREE **NUT-FREE** **SOY-FREE** **5 OR FEWER INGREDIENTS** **QUICK**

PREP TIME: 5 minutes **COOK SETTING:** High Pressure for 7 minutes, Sauté for 3 to 4 minutes **RELEASE:** Quick **TOTAL TIME:** 20 minutes

These potatoes come out of the Instant Pot perfectly fluffy and delicious. I use baby potatoes in this recipe, but any red- or yellow-skinned potatoes work if you cut them into 2-inch chunks. Feel free to add more herbs to your liking, such as oregano, marjoram, chives, or dill. You can also turn this classic side dish into a meal by adding some steamed broccoli and tossing it with the potatoes and herbs. **Serves 4 to 6**

2 pounds baby red-skinned potatoes

1 cup water

3 tablespoons plant-based butter, melted, or extra-virgin olive oil

1 teaspoon garlic powder

1 teaspoon dried thyme

1 teaspoon dried rosemary, crushed

1 teaspoon salt

Freshly ground black pepper

1. Pierce the potatoes with a fork and slice any larger potatoes in half. In your Instant Pot, combine the potatoes and water. Lock the lid and turn the steam release handle to Sealing. Using the Pressure Cook/Manual function, set the cooker to High Pressure for 7 minutes.

2. When the cook time is complete, quick-release the pressure and carefully remove the lid. Drain the water and select the Sauté function. Add the butter or olive oil, garlic powder, thyme, rosemary, salt, and pepper to taste. Stir to combine and allow the potatoes to brown slightly for 3 to 4 minutes.

WFPB TIP: Omit the plant-based butter or oil and substitute 3 tablespoons of vegetable broth to sauté the potatoes. Omit the salt.

PER SERVING: Calories: 251; Fat: 10g; Protein: 4g; Total Carbs: 37g; Fiber: 4g; Sugar: 3g; Sodium: 623mg

Creamed Spinach

GLUTEN-FREE **WFPB** **QUICK**

PREP TIME: 10 minutes **COOK SETTING:** Sauté for 3 to 5 minutes, High Pressure for 5 minutes **RELEASE:** Natural for 5 minutes, then quick **TOTAL TIME:** 25 minutes

Nothing says "fancy restaurant side dish" to me like creamed spinach. With this recipe, you don't even have to leave the house to enjoy this tasty side—and it's done in less than 30 minutes. **Serves 4 to 6**

½ medium onion, diced

4 garlic cloves, minced

1 (16-ounce) package frozen chopped spinach

1¾ cups unsweetened plant-based milk, divided

1 cup water

¾ cup raw cashews

1 tablespoon freshly squeezed lemon juice

1 teaspoon chickpea miso paste

½ teaspoon ground or freshly grated nutmeg

Freshly ground black pepper

FLAVOR BOOST: Add some crunch to the spinach with a can of drained and chopped water chestnuts. You can also add a 14-ounce can of drained quartered artichoke hearts to the spinach mixture before pressure-cooking.

1. Select the Sauté function on your Instant Pot and allow it to preheat for 2 minutes. Sauté the onion until translucent, 3 to 5 minutes, adding water as needed to prevent sticking. Add the garlic and sauté for 30 seconds. Cancel the Sauté function, then add the spinach and 1¼ cups of the milk. Lock the lid and turn the steam release handle to Sealing. Using the Pressure Cook/Manual function, set the cooker to High Pressure for 5 minutes.

2. Boil the water and, using a large bowl, pour it over the cashews; let soak for at least 30 minutes before draining. If you have a high-speed blender, you can skip this step and soaking.

3. In a blender or food processor, combine the drained cashews, the remaining ½ cup of milk, the lemon juice, miso, nutmeg, and pepper to taste. Blend until smooth.

4. When the cook time is complete, let the pressure release naturally for 5 minutes; quick-release any remaining pressure and carefully remove the lid. Combine the sauce with the spinach. Serve immediately.

PER SERVING: Calories: 237; Fat: 14g; Protein: 13g; Total Carbs: 19g; Fiber: 5g; Sugar: 6g; Sodium: 193mg

Savory Polenta with Mushroom Ragù

GLUTEN-FREE WFPB

PREP TIME: 5 minutes **COOK SETTING:** Sauté for 16 to 18 minutes, High Pressure for 10 minutes **RELEASE:** Quick **TOTAL TIME:** 35 minutes

This savory, Italian-inspired side dish is a wonderful way to prepare polenta. Add a tossed salad to turn it into a meal. *Serves 4 to 6*

1 medium onion, diced

1⅓ cups Easy Vegetable Broth (page 108) or no-salt-added vegetable broth, divided, plus more as needed

2 garlic cloves, minced

8 ounces white button mushrooms, sliced

8 ounces cremini mushrooms, sliced

3 tablespoons tomato paste

2 teaspoons dried thyme

1 teaspoon balsamic vinegar

Freshly ground black pepper

3 cups water

1 cup polenta or coarsely ground cornmeal

1 cup unsweetened plant-based milk

FLAVOR BOOST: Stir ½ cup of grated plant-based parmesan into the polenta after cooking along with 2 tablespoons of plant-based butter.

1. Select the Sauté function on your Instant Pot and allow it to preheat for 2 minutes. Sauté the onion until translucent, 3 to 5 minutes, adding broth as needed to prevent it from sticking. Add the garlic and cook for 30 seconds. Add the mushrooms and sauté about 5 minutes, until softened. Stir in the tomato paste, thyme, vinegar, and pepper to taste. Add ⅓ cup of the broth and scrape up any browned bits from the bottom of the pot. Bring to a simmer and cook for 3 minutes. Cancel the Sauté function and remove the mushroom mixture to a small bowl. Rinse and dry the inner pot.

2. Select the Sauté function on your Instant Pot, then combine the water, polenta, milk, and the remaining 1 cup of broth, whisking continuously, for 5 minutes. When the mixture reaches a simmer, cancel the Sauté function. Lock the lid and turn the steam release handle to Sealing. Using the Pressure Cook/Manual function, set the cooker to High Pressure for 10 minutes.

3. When the cook time is complete, quick-release the pressure and carefully remove the lid. Stir, then transfer to a serving bowl and top with the mushroom ragù. Serve immediately.

PER SERVING: Calories: 221; Fat: 2g; Protein: 9g; Total Carbs: 43g; Fiber: 4g; Sugar: 7g; Sodium: 47mg

Red Quinoa and Black Bean Chili, page 51

CHAPTER 4
Soups, Stews, and Chilis

Broccoli-Cheeze Soup

GLUTEN-FREE **SOY-FREE** **WFPB**

PREP TIME: 15 minutes **COOK SETTING:** Sauté for 3 to 5 minutes, High Pressure for 3 minutes **RELEASE:** Natural for 10 minutes, then quick **TOTAL TIME:** 40 minutes

To get the creamiest result, make the extra effort to puree this soup in a countertop blender rather than using an immersion blender. So decadent and smooth! *Serves 4 to 6*

1 pound broccoli

1 medium onion, diced

5 cups Easy Vegetable Broth (page 108) or no-salt-added vegetable broth

3 medium yellow potatoes, diced (about 3 cups)

2 large carrots, chopped into ½-inch round pieces (about 1 cup)

4 garlic cloves, crushed

½ cup raw cashews

3 tablespoons nutritional yeast

1 tablespoon chickpea miso paste

1. Separate the broccoli stalks from the florets and dice the stalks; set aside. Cut the florets into bite-size pieces and set aside in a medium bowl.

2. Select the Sauté function on your Instant Pot. Sauté the onion for 3 to 5 minutes. Cancel the Sauté setting, then stir in the diced stalks, broth, potatoes, carrots, garlic, cashews, nutritional yeast, and miso, scraping up any browned bits from the bottom of the pot. Lock the lid and turn the steam release handle to Sealing. Using the Pressure Cook/Manual function, set the cooker to High Pressure for 3 minutes.

3. When the cook time is complete, let the pressure release naturally for 10 minutes; quick-release any remaining pressure and carefully remove the lid.

4. Ladle the soup into a blender in batches and blend until smooth and creamy. Put the broccoli florets in a large heatproof bowl. Pour the hot blended soup over the florets. Serve immediately. Store any leftovers in the fridge for up to 4 days in a covered container.

INGREDIENT TIP: Using miso made from chickpeas rather than soybeans makes this recipe soy-free. The miso adds a salty umami flavor to this soup.

PER SERVING: Calories: 397; Fat: 9g; Protein: 13g; Total Carbs: 71g; Fiber: 11g; Sugar: 8g; Sodium: 241mg

Chickpea, Farro, and Tomato Stew

NUT-FREE **SOY-FREE** **WFPB** **ONE-POT MEAL** **WORTH THE WAIT**

PREP TIME: 10 minutes **COOK SETTING:** Sauté for 3 to 5 minutes, High Pressure for 10 minutes **RELEASE:** Natural for 10 minutes, then quick **TOTAL TIME:** 50 minutes

Serve up this Italian-inspired one-pot meal with a hunk of crusty bread to sop up the flavorful tomato sauce. This hearty, healthy stew is my idea of culinary heaven. *Serves 4 to 6*

1 medium onion, diced

5 garlic cloves, minced

1 tablespoon no-salt-added Italian seasoning

¼ to ½ teaspoon red pepper flakes

3 cups Easy Vegetable Broth (page 108), no-salt-added vegetable broth, or water

1 cup pearled farro

1 (28-ounce) can no-salt-added diced tomatoes

1 (15-ounce) can no-salt-added chickpeas, drained and rinsed

5 ounces baby spinach

Zest and juice of 1 lemon

Freshly ground black pepper

Salt (optional)

Plant-based parmesan (optional), for serving

1. Select the Sauté function on your Instant Pot. Sauté the onion for 3 to 5 minutes, adding water as needed, a tablespoon at a time, to prevent sticking. Add the garlic, Italian seasoning, and red pepper flakes to taste, and stir for 30 seconds, until fragrant. Cancel the Sauté function, then add the broth, farro, tomatoes, and chickpeas. Lock the lid and turn the steam release handle to Sealing. Using the Pressure Cook/Manual function, set the cooker to High Pressure for 10 minutes.

2. When the cook time is complete, let the pressure release naturally for 10 minutes; quick-release any remaining pressure and carefully remove the lid. Stir in the spinach and lemon zest and juice, allowing the residual heat from the stew to wilt the spinach. Season to taste with pepper and salt (if using). Serve immediately with a sprinkle of plant-based parmesan, if desired. Store any leftovers in the fridge for up to 4 days in a covered container.

FLAVOR BOOST: Place each serving in an oven-safe bowl and sprinkle with plant-based mozzarella. Briefly bake or broil the stew to melt the cheeze.

PER SERVING: Calories: 336; Fat: 3g; Protein: 14g; Total Carbs: 68g; Fiber: 18g; Sugar: 10g; Sodium: 59mg

Roasted Red Pepper Soup

GLUTEN-FREE **SOY-FREE** **WFPB** **ONE-POT MEAL** **WORTH THE WAIT**

PREP TIME: 10 minutes **COOK SETTING:** Sauté for 3 to 5 minutes, High Pressure for 6 minutes **RELEASE:** Natural for 10 minutes, then quick **TOTAL TIME:** 45 minutes

Comforting with a kick, this is my husband's favorite soup. The hint of sweetness from the maple syrup combined with the flavor and anti-oxidant properties of the turmeric may make this soup your family's favorite, too! **Serves 4 to 6**

1 medium onion, diced

4 garlic cloves, smashed

¼ teaspoon red pepper flakes (optional)

2½ cups water

2 (12-ounce) jars roasted red peppers, drained

1 (28-ounce) can no-salt-added crushed tomatoes

1 (6-ounce) can no-salt-added tomato paste

1 tablespoon dried dill

1 tablespoon maple syrup

2 teaspoons garlic powder

1 teaspoon ground turmeric

1 (14-ounce) can full-fat coconut milk

Freshly ground black pepper

Salt (optional)

1. Select the Sauté function on your Instant Pot. Sauté the onion for 3 to 5 minutes, adding water as needed, a tablespoon at a time, to prevent sticking. Add the garlic and red pepper flakes (if using) and sauté until fragrant, about 30 seconds.

2. Cancel the Sauté function and add the water, red peppers, tomatoes, tomato paste, dill, maple syrup, garlic powder, and turmeric. Stir well to combine. Lock the lid and turn the steam release handle to Sealing. Using the Pressure Cook/Manual function, set the cooker to High Pressure for 6 minutes.

3. When the cook time is complete, let the pressure release naturally for 10 minutes; quick-release any remaining pressure and carefully remove the lid.

4. Stir in the coconut milk and season to taste with pepper and salt (if using). Serve immediately. Store any leftovers in the fridge for up to 4 days in a covered container.

VARIATION TIP: This recipe easily becomes Tomato Basil Soup by eliminating the red peppers and substituting dried basil for the dill.

PER SERVING: Calories: 319; Fat: 22g; Protein: 7g; Total Carbs: 31g; Fiber: 8g; Sugar: 18g; Sodium: 346mg

Red Quinoa and Black Bean Chili

GLUTEN-FREE **NUT-FREE** **SOY-FREE** **WFPB** **ONE-POT MEAL**

PREP TIME: 10 minutes **COOK SETTING:** Sauté for 3 to 5 minutes, High Pressure for 7 minutes **RELEASE:** Natural for 10 minutes, then quick **TOTAL TIME:** 35 minutes

Quinoa is a grain that comes in red, black, and white varieties. I prefer the nuttiness and firmer texture of the red, as well as its deep color in this dish, but any type will do. I like to serve this chili with a generous dollop of guacamole on top. **Serves 4 to 6**

1 large onion, diced

2 bell peppers, diced

4 garlic cloves, minced

1 tablespoon gluten-free chili powder

2 teaspoons ground cumin

2 cups water

2 (14.5-ounce) cans no-salt-added black beans, drained and rinsed

1 (28-ounce) can no-salt-added diced tomatoes

½ cup red quinoa

1 tablespoon gluten-free vegan Worcestershire sauce

Freshly ground black pepper

Salt (optional)

1. Select the Sauté function on your Instant Pot. Sauté the onion and bell peppers for 3 to 5 minutes, adding water as needed, a tablespoon at a time, to prevent sticking. Add the garlic, chili powder, and cumin and stir for 30 seconds, until fragrant. Add the water, black beans, tomatoes, quinoa, and Worcestershire sauce and season to taste with pepper and salt (if using). Cancel the Sauté function.

2. Lock the lid and turn the steam release handle to Sealing. Using the Pressure Cook/Manual function, set the cooker to High Pressure for 7 minutes.

3. When the cook time is complete, let the pressure release naturally for 10 minutes; quick-release any remaining pressure and carefully remove the lid. Stir and serve immediately. Store any leftovers in the fridge for up to 4 days in a covered container.

FLAVOR BOOST: For a kick of heat, add a chopped jalapeño pepper or 2 to 3 chopped canned chipotles in adobo when stirring in the garlic and spices.

PER SERVING: Calories: 324; Fat: 3g; Protein: 18g; Total Carbs: 61g; Fiber: 19g; Sugar: 9g; Sodium: 127mg

Rich Mushroom Soup

GLUTEN-FREE **WFPB**

PREP TIME: 10 minutes **COOK SETTING:** Sauté for 8 to 10 minutes, High Pressure for 5 minutes **RELEASE:** Natural for 5 minutes, then quick **TOTAL TIME:** 35 minutes

When it comes to plant-based home cooking, mushrooms are amazingly versatile. This soup is partially pureed for a rich, creamy broth with mushrooms in every bite. I like to serve it with a dollop of Soy Yogurt (page 21). **Serves 4 to 6**

1 medium onion, diced

1 pound mushrooms, roughly chopped

4 garlic cloves, crushed

2 thyme sprigs, or 1 teaspoon dried

3 cups Easy Vegetable Broth (page 108) or no-salt-added vegetable broth

1 tablespoon chickpea miso paste

1 tablespoon gluten-free vegan Worcestershire sauce

1 cup unsweetened plant-based milk

1 tablespoon arrowroot starch or gluten-free flour blend

Freshly ground black pepper

Salt (optional)

1. Select the Sauté function on your Instant Pot. Sauté the onion for 3 to 5 minutes until translucent, adding water as needed, a tablespoon at a time, to prevent sticking. Stir in the mushrooms, garlic, and thyme and sauté for 5 minutes. Cancel the Sauté setting and add the broth, miso, and Worcestershire sauce. Lock the lid and turn the steam release handle to Sealing. Using the Pressure Cook/Manual function, set the cooker to High Pressure for 5 minutes.

2. When the cook time is complete, let the pressure release naturally for 5 minutes; quick-release any remaining pressure and carefully remove the lid. Discard the thyme stems.

3. Set aside 2 cups of the soup. In a blender, puree the remaining soup. Select the Sauté function. Whisk the milk and arrowroot into the soup until boiling and slightly thickened. Add the reserved soup back into the pot and stir well to combine. Serve immediately. Store any leftovers in the fridge for up to 4 days in a covered container.

INGREDIENT TIP: For this soup, feel free to choose any type of mushroom you love best. I often combine whatever I have in the fridge rather than using just one type.

PER SERVING: Calories: 84; Fat: 2g; Protein: 6g; Total Carbs: 13g; Fiber: 2g; Sugar: 6g; Sodium: 237mg

White Bean Chili Verde

GLUTEN-FREE   NUT-FREE   SOY-FREE   WFPB   ONE-POT MEAL   WORTH THE WAIT

PREP TIME: 10 minutes   **COOK SETTING:** Sauté for 6 to 10 minutes, High Pressure for 45 minutes   **RELEASE:** Natural for 10 minutes, then quick   **TOTAL TIME:** 1 hour 20 minutes

Spicy and satisfying, this soup gets its bright shades of green from celery, chile peppers, and spinach. The color combined with the creaminess of the beans make this chili a winner. **Serves 4 to 6**

1 large onion, diced

4 celery stalks, diced

6 cups Easy Vegetable Broth (page 108) or no-salt-added vegetable broth, divided

2 jalapeño peppers, minced

5 garlic cloves, minced

1 tablespoon ground cumin

2 teaspoons dried oregano

1 pound dried great northern beans (about 2 cups), rinsed and sorted

2 (7-ounce) cans diced green chiles

5 ounces fresh baby spinach

Freshly ground black pepper

Salt (optional)

1. Select the Sauté function on your Instant Pot. Sauté the onion and celery for 3 to 5 minutes, until translucent, adding broth as needed to prevent sticking. Add the jalapeños, garlic, cumin, and oregano and stir for 30 seconds, until fragrant. Add the remaining broth, beans, and green chiles. Stir to combine, scraping up any bits from the bottom of the pot. Sauté for 3 to 5 minutes, then cancel the Sauté function.

2. Lock the lid and turn the steam release handle to Sealing. Using the Pressure Cook/Manual function, set the cooker to High Pressure for 45 minutes.

3. When the cook time is complete, let the pressure release naturally for 10 minutes; quick-release any remaining pressure and carefully remove the lid. Using an immersion blender, puree some of the chili to thicken it, leaving some unpureed. Stir in the spinach until wilted. Season to taste with pepper and salt (if using). Serve immediately. Store any leftovers in the fridge for up to 4 days in a covered container.

FLAVOR BOOST: Try garnishing this chili with chopped scallions, diced avocado, freshly squeezed lime juice, and chopped fresh cilantro.

PER SERVING: Calories: 446; Fat: 2g; Protein: 28g; Total Carbs: 83g; Fiber: 27g; Sugar: 5g; Sodium: 356mg

Smoky and Sweet Butternut Squash Soup

GLUTEN-FREE **NUT-FREE** **SOY-FREE** **WFPB** **WORTH THE WAIT**

PREP TIME: 15 minutes **COOK SETTING:** Sauté for 3 to 5 minutes, High Pressure for 15 minutes **RELEASE:** Quick **TOTAL TIME:** 45 minutes

In this recipe, butternut squash soup gets a hint of sweetness from the apple and a touch of smokiness from the paprika. Cauliflower lends extra fiber, body, and creaminess, and turmeric adds gorgeous color and anti-inflammatory properties to boot. Like many of my blended soups, I enjoy this with a dollop of Soy Yogurt (page 21). **Serves 4 to 6**

1 medium onion, diced

3 cups Easy Vegetable Broth (page 108) or no-salt-added vegetable broth, divided

3 garlic cloves, crushed

1-inch knob fresh turmeric, peeled and grated, or 1 teaspoon ground turmeric

2 teaspoons smoked paprika

1 small butternut squash, peeled and cubed into 1-inch chunks (1½ to 2 cups)

1 small cauliflower, chopped (3 to 4 cups)

1 medium apple (any sweet variety such as Gala or Fuji), cored and chopped

Salt (optional)

1. Select the Sauté function on your Instant Pot. Sauté the onion 3 to 5 minutes, until translucent, adding broth as needed, a tablespoon at a time, to prevent sticking. Add the garlic, turmeric, and paprika and stir until fragrant, about 30 seconds.

2. Add the remaining broth and scrape up any bits from the bottom of the pot. Cancel the Sauté setting and add the butternut squash, cauliflower, and apple. Lock the lid and turn the steam release handle to Sealing. Using the Pressure Cook/Manual function, set the cooker to High Pressure for 15 minutes.

3. When the cook time is complete, quick-release the pressure and carefully remove the lid. Using an immersion blender, puree the soup until smooth. Season to taste with salt (if using). Serve immediately. Store leftovers in the fridge for up to 4 days in a covered container.

INGREDIENT TIP: Smoked paprika is this soup's secret ingredient, but if you don't like the smoky flavor, use a sweet or hot paprika instead.

PER SERVING: Calories: 139; Fat: 1g; Protein: 4g; Total Carbs: 34g; Fiber: 7g; Sugar: 11g; Sodium: 30mg

Coconut-Cabbage Stew

GLUTEN-FREE **WFPB** **ONE-POT MEAL** **QUICK**

PREP TIME: 10 minutes **COOK SETTING:** Sauté for 3 to 5 minutes, High Pressure for 3 minutes **RELEASE:** Natural for 5 minutes, then quick **TOTAL TIME:** 30 minutes

This Thai-inspired stew full of cabbage melds perfectly with rich coconut milk—especially if you add a dash of Hot Pepper Sauce (page 112) when serving. To supercharge the protein, add some drained, cubed extra-firm tofu before adding the cabbage. **Serves 4 to 6**

1 medium onion, diced

8 ounces shiitake or cremini mushrooms, chopped

4 garlic cloves, minced

1 (1-inch) knob fresh ginger, peeled and grated, or 1 teaspoon dried ginger

3 large carrots, diced

2 or 3 medium yellow potatoes, chopped into 1-inch chunks

1 tablespoon gluten-free soy sauce

2½ to 3 cups Easy Vegetable Broth (page 108) or no-salt-added vegetable broth

1 small head green or napa cabbage, sliced

1 (14-ounce) can full-fat coconut milk

Freshly ground black pepper

1. Select the Sauté function on your Instant Pot. Sauté the onion and mushrooms for 3 to 5 minutes, until the onion is translucent, adding water as needed to prevent sticking. Add the garlic and ginger and stir for 30 seconds, until fragrant. Cancel the Sauté function, then stir in the carrots, potatoes, and soy sauce. Stir in 2½ cups of broth and add more as needed to just cover the vegetables. Place the cabbage on top. Lock the lid and turn the steam release handle to Sealing. Using the Pressure Cook/Manual function, set the cooker to High Pressure for 3 minutes.

2. When the cook time is complete, let the pressure release naturally for 5 minutes; quick-release any remaining pressure and carefully remove the lid. Stir in the coconut milk until heated through and season to taste with pepper. Serve immediately. Store any leftovers in the fridge for up to 4 days in a covered container.

FLAVOR BOOST: Top each bowl with a handful of fresh bean sprouts, chopped scallions, chopped fresh cilantro, and a squeeze of lime juice.

PER SERVING: Calories: 440; Fat: 22g; Protein: 10g; Total Carbs: 58g; Fiber: 11g; Sugar: 12g; Sodium: 234mg

Wild Rice Soup

GLUTEN-FREE **NUT-FREE** **SOY-FREE** **WFPB** **ONE-POT MEAL** **WORTH THE WAIT**

PREP TIME: 10 minutes **COOK SETTING:** Sauté for 3 to 5 minutes, High Pressure for 50 minutes **RELEASE:** Natural for 10 minutes, then quick **TOTAL TIME:** 1 hour 30 minutes

This hearty soup borders on a stew with loads of textures and flavors. From the nutty and toothsome wild rice to the creamy chickpeas, the savory broth brings everything together. **Serves 4 to 6**

1 medium onion, diced

3 large carrots, diced

4 celery stalks, diced

3 garlic cloves, minced

1 teaspoon no-salt-added poultry seasoning

1 cup wild rice

6½ cups Easy Vegetable Broth (page 108) or no-salt-added vegetable broth

1 cup dried chickpeas, rinsed and sorted

1 bay leaf

3 to 4 ounces baby spinach

Freshly ground black pepper

Salt (optional)

1. Select the Sauté function on your Instant Pot. Sauté the onion for 3 to 5 minutes, until translucent, adding water as needed to prevent sticking. Stir in the carrots, celery, garlic, and poultry seasoning and sauté about 30 seconds. Stir in the rice. Cancel the Sauté setting and add the broth, chickpeas, and bay leaf, scraping up any browned bits from the bottom of the pot. Lock the lid and turn the steam release handle to Sealing. Using the Pressure Cook/Manual function, set the cooker to High Pressure for 50 minutes.

2. When the cook time is complete, let the pressure release naturally for 10 minutes; quick-release any remaining pressure and carefully remove the lid. Remove and discard the bay leaf.

3. Add the spinach and stir until wilted. Season to taste with the pepper and salt (if using). Serve immediately. Store any leftovers in the fridge for up to 4 days in a covered container.

INGREDIENT TIP: Don't mistake wild rice for black rice, which will turn the whole pot a less-than-appetizing color. You can also use a wild rice blend without changing the liquid amount or cooking time.

PER SERVING: Calories: 377; Fat: 4g; Protein: 18g; Total Carbs: 73g; Fiber: 11g; Sugar: 10g; Sodium: 87mg

Sweet Potato and Peanut Stew with Kale

GLUTEN-FREE   SOY-FREE   WFPB   ONE-POT MEAL   WORTH THE WAIT

PREP TIME: 15 minutes   **COOK SETTING:** Sauté for 3 to 5 minutes, High Pressure for 10 minutes   **RELEASE:** Natural for 10 minutes, then quick   **TOTAL TIME:** 55 minutes

Inspired by a dish common in Central and West Africa, this satisfying stew features a thick sauce made with tomatoes and peanut butter. Be sure to scrape up any browned bits from the bottom of the pot before pressure-cooking to avoid a burn notice.   **Serves 4 to 6**

1 medium onion, diced

4 garlic cloves, minced

1 (1-inch) knob ginger, peeled and grated

1 teaspoon ground turmeric

1 teaspoon ground cumin

2 (14-ounce) cans no-salt-added fire-roasted tomatoes

3 medium sweet potatoes, peeled and chopped into 1½-inch chunks

2 cups warm water

¾ cup unsalted smooth peanut butter

5 ounces kale, chopped

Freshly ground black pepper

Salt (optional)

¾ cup chopped unsalted peanuts

1. Select the Sauté function on your Instant Pot and sauté the onion for 3 to 5 minutes. Add the garlic, ginger, turmeric, and cumin and sauté for 30 seconds, until fragrant. Cancel the Sauté function and add the tomatoes, scraping any bits off the bottom of the pot. Add the sweet potatoes.

2. In a medium bowl, whisk together the water and peanut butter to blend. Stir into the pot. Top with the kale. Lock the lid and turn the steam release handle to Sealing. Using the Pressure Cook/Manual function, set the cooker to High Pressure for 10 minutes.

3. When the cook time is complete, let the pressure release naturally for 10 minutes; quick-release any remaining pressure and carefully remove the lid. Season to taste with pepper and salt (if using), garnish with the peanuts, and serve immediately. Store leftovers in the fridge for up to 4 days in a covered container.

VARIATION TIPS: Use Swiss chard, spinach, or napa cabbage in place of the kale. Stir in a cup of coconut milk at the end for a creamier stew.

PER SERVING: Calories: 603; Fat: 40g; Protein: 23g; Total Carbs: 51g; Fiber: 14g; Sugar: 18g; Sodium: 121mg

Quick Barbecue Chili

GLUTEN-FREE **NUT-FREE** **SOY-FREE** **WFPB** **ONE-POT MEAL** **WORTH THE WAIT**

PREP TIME: 10 minutes **COOK SETTING:** Sauté for 3 to 5 minutes, High Pressure for 10 minutes **RELEASE:** Natural for 10 minutes, then quick **TOTAL TIME:** 50 minutes

The sweetness of the barbecue sauce in this chili is a pleasantly unexpected flavor. If you don't have time to make your own barbecue sauce, you can use your favorite bottled sauce in a pinch. *Serves 4 to 6*

1 large onion, diced

1 bell pepper, diced

4 garlic cloves, minced

2 teaspoons ground cumin

2 teaspoons smoked paprika

2½ cups water

2 (14.5-ounce) cans no-salt-added kidney beans, drained and rinsed

1 (28-ounce) can no-salt-added diced tomatoes

½ cup millet

¼ cup Sweet and Tangy Maple Barbecue Sauce (page 110) or your favorite store-bought brand

Freshly ground black pepper

Salt (optional)

1. Select the Sauté function on your Instant Pot. Sauté the onion and bell pepper for 3 to 5 minutes, until the onion is translucent, adding water as needed to prevent sticking. Add the garlic, cumin, and paprika and stir for 30 seconds, until fragrant. Cancel the Sauté function. Add the water, kidney beans, tomatoes, millet, and barbecue sauce and season to taste with pepper and salt (if using).

2. Lock the lid and turn the steam release handle to Sealing. Using the Pressure Cook/Manual function, set the cooker to High Pressure for 10 minutes.

3. When the cook time is complete, let the pressure release naturally for 10 minutes; quick-release any remaining pressure and carefully remove the lid. Serve immediately. Store leftovers in the fridge for up to 4 days in a covered container.

LEFTOVERS TIP: Stir leftover chili into your favorite plant-based macaroni and cheeze for a delicious chili mac meal.

PER SERVING: Calories: 361; Fat: 3g; Protein: 17g; Total Carbs: 70g; Fiber: 16g; Sugar: 14g; Sodium: 212mg

Curried Cauliflower Soup

GLUTEN-FREE   NUT-FREE   SOY-FREE   WFPB   WORTH THE WAIT

PREP TIME: 10 minutes   **COOK SETTING:** Sauté for 3 to 5 minutes, High Pressure for 7 minutes   **RELEASE:** Natural for 10 minutes, then quick   **TOTAL TIME:** 45 minutes

Thick, rich, and spicy, thanks to the curry powder, this soup has a surprising depth of flavor given the short ingredient list. I like to serve it with a cooling dollop of Soy Yogurt (page 21). **Serves 4 to 6**

1 medium onion, chopped

3 garlic cloves, minced

1 tablespoon curry powder

3 cups Easy Vegetable Broth (page 108) or no-salt-added vegetable broth

1 head cauliflower, roughly chopped

2 medium yellow potatoes, chopped

Freshly ground black pepper

Salt (optional)

1. Select the Sauté function on your Instant Pot. Sauté the onion for 3 to 5 minutes, until translucent, adding water as needed to prevent sticking. Add the garlic and curry powder and stir for 30 seconds, until fragrant. Cancel the Sauté function and add the broth, scraping up any browned bits from the bottom of the pot. Stir in the cauliflower and potatoes and season to taste with pepper and salt (if using). Lock the lid and turn the steam release handle to Sealing. Using the Pressure Cook/Manual function, set the cooker to High Pressure for 7 minutes.

2. When the cook time is complete, let the pressure release naturally for 10 minutes; quick-release any remaining pressure and carefully remove the lid.

3. Using an immersion blender, carefully puree the soup in the pot. Serve immediately. Store any leftovers in the fridge for up to 4 days in a covered container.

INGREDIENT TIP: Fresh cauliflower is easy enough to quickly break down, but you can use a package of frozen cauliflower florets in place of the fresh if you're in a big hurry. No need to defrost!

PER SERVING: Calories: 198; Fat: 1g; Protein: 7g; Total Carbs: 44g; Fiber: 8g; Sugar: 5g; Sodium: 57mg

Barley, Mushroom, and Kale Stew

NUT-FREE   SOY-FREE   WFPB   ONE-POT MEAL   WORTH THE WAIT

PREP TIME: 10 minutes   **COOK SETTING:** Sauté for 3 to 5 minutes, High Pressure for 20 minutes   **RELEASE:** Natural for 10 minutes, then quick   **TOTAL TIME:** 1 hour

Hearty, thick, and tangy because of the balsamic vinegar and tomato paste, this stick-to-your-ribs stew is a one-pot meal your whole family will enjoy.   **Serves 4 to 6**

1 medium onion, diced

4 celery stalks, diced

1 pound cremini mushrooms, sliced

3 garlic cloves, minced

2 tablespoons tomato paste

1 tablespoon no-salt-added poultry seasoning

6 cups Easy Vegetable Broth (page 108), no-salt-added vegetable broth, or water

1 cup pearled barley

2 tablespoons balsamic vinegar

1 tablespoon chickpea miso paste

1 bunch kale, stemmed and chopped

Freshly ground black pepper

Salt (optional)

1. Select the Sauté function on your Instant Pot. Sauté the onion, celery, and mushrooms for 3 to 5 minutes, until the onion is translucent, adding water as needed to prevent sticking. Add the garlic, tomato paste, and poultry seasoning and stir for 30 seconds, until fragrant. Stir in the broth, barley, vinegar, and miso, scraping up any bits from the bottom of the pot. Place the kale on top. Cancel the Sauté function.

2. Lock the lid and turn the steam release handle to Sealing. Using the Pressure Cook/Manual function, set the cooker to High Pressure for 20 minutes.

3. When the cook time is complete, let the pressure release naturally for 10 minutes; quick-release any remaining pressure and carefully remove the lid. Stir well and season to taste with pepper and salt (if using). Serve immediately. Store any leftovers in the fridge for up to 4 days in a covered container.

INGREDIENT TIP: Look for the more common pearled barley to use in this recipe rather than the unpearled variety. If you prefer a gluten-free option, try sorghum in the same measurements.

PER SERVING: Calories: 248; Fat: 1g; Protein: 11g; Total Carbs: 52g; Fiber: 11g; Sugar: 7g; Sodium: 196mg

Cowboy Caviar, page 70

CHAPTER 5

Beans, Grains, and Legumes

Coconut Brown Rice

GLUTEN-FREE SOY-FREE WFPB 5 OR FEWER INGREDIENTS WORTH THE WAIT

PREP TIME: 5 minutes **COOK SETTING:** High Pressure for 22 minutes **RELEASE:** Natural for 10 minutes, then quick **TOTAL TIME:** 45 minutes

Aromatic basmati rice is common in Indian and Pakistani cooking, and I love brown rice for the toothsome nuttiness it brings to a dish. Much of the nutrition in brown rice, including the fiber and protein, comes from the outer layer called the bran. Keeping that bran intact is what makes brown rice a whole food. *Serves 4 to 6*

2 cups brown basmati rice, rinsed well to remove the starch

1 cup water

1 (14-ounce) can full-fat coconut milk

2 scallions, white and green parts, diced (optional)

Salt (optional)

1. In your Instant Pot, combine the rice, water, and coconut milk. Lock the lid and turn the steam release handle to Sealing. Using the Pressure Cook/Manual function, set the cooker to High Pressure for 22 minutes.

2. When the cook time is complete, let the pressure release naturally for 10 minutes; quick-release any remaining pressure and carefully remove the lid. If using, add the scallions and salt to taste. Fluff with a fork to combine. Serve immediately.

VARIATION TIP: If you prefer to use white basmati rice, reduce the cook time to 6 minutes.

PER SERVING: Calories: 538; Fat: 24g; Protein: 9g; Total Carbs: 74g; Fiber: 3g; Sugar: 1g; Sodium: 19mg

Tabouleh Salad

NUT-FREE **SOY-FREE** **QUICK**

PREP TIME: 5 minutes **COOK SETTING:** High Pressure for 0 minutes **RELEASE:** Natural for 2 minutes, then quick **TOTAL TIME:** 20 minutes

Here's a refreshing recipe to make during the height of summer using the bounty of fresh produce from your garden or the farmers' market. Yes, there's a lot of chopping, but you can get everything done while you're waiting for the bulgur to cook and cool. **Serves 4 to 6**

1 cup water

¾ cup red bulgur wheat
  (such as Bob's Red
  Mill brand)

½ teaspoon garlic powder

1 cup chopped
  flat-leaf parsley

¼ cup chopped
  mint leaves

4 scallions, white and
  green parts, diced

2 tomatoes, diced

1 cucumber, peeled
  and diced

Zest and juice of 1 lemon

2 to 4 tablespoons
  extra-virgin olive oil
  (optional)

Freshly ground
  black pepper

Salt (optional)

1. In your Instant Pot, combine the water, bulgur, and garlic powder. Lock the lid and turn the steam release handle to Sealing. Using the Pressure Cook/Manual function, set the cooker to High Pressure for 0 minutes. (The food will cook as the pot comes up to pressure.)

2. When the cook time is complete, let the pressure release naturally for 2 minutes; quick-release any remaining pressure and carefully remove the lid. Remove the bulgur to a large bowl and let cool over an ice bath.

3. In a large mixing bowl, combine the parsley, mint, scallions, tomatoes, cucumber, lemon zest and juice, and cooled bulgur. Drizzle with olive oil (if using) and season to taste with pepper and salt (if using). Stir well to combine. Serve immediately.

VARIATION TIP: To make this dish gluten-free, substitute ½ cup quinoa for the bulgur wheat and cook with ¾ cup water for 1 minute on High Pressure.

PER SERVING: Calories: 129; Fat: 1g; Protein: 5g; Total Carbs: 29g; Fiber: 6g; Sugar: 4g; Sodium: 22mg

Cilantro-Lime Brown Rice

GLUTEN-FREE **NUT-FREE** **SOY-FREE** **WFPB** **5 OR FEWER INGREDIENTS** **QUICK**

PREP TIME: 5 minutes **COOK SETTING:** High Pressure for 15 minutes **RELEASE:** Natural for 5 minutes, then quick **TOTAL TIME:** 30 minutes

When you're looking for the ideal hands-off side to go with your next Mexican, Indian, Chinese, or Thai dish, look no further. This rice cooks up perfectly, and the addition of cilantro and lime brings a bright pop of flavor and color. **Serves 4 to 6**

2 cups brown rice

1¼ cups water

1¼ cups Easy Vegetable Broth (page 108) or no-salt-added vegetable broth

3 garlic cloves, minced

Zest and juice of 1 lime

1 small bunch cilantro, chopped

1. In your Instant Pot, combine the rice, water, broth, and garlic. Lock the lid and turn the steam release handle to Sealing. Using the Pressure Cook/Manual function, set the cooker to High Pressure for 15 minutes.

2. When the cook time is complete, let the pressure release naturally for 5 minutes; quick-release any remaining pressure and carefully remove the lid. Add the lime zest and juice and cilantro. Fluff with a fork to combine. Serve immediately. Store any leftovers in the fridge for up to 4 days in a covered container.

INGREDIENT TIP: Cilantro stems are delicious, so don't discard them. They add a lot of flavor and a little more texture.

PER SERVING: Calories: 350; Fat: 3g; Protein: 7g; Total Carbs: 74g; Fiber: 3g; Sugar: 1g; Sodium: 5mg

Mediterranean Millet Salad

GLUTEN-FREE   **NUT-FREE**   **SOY-FREE**   **WFPB**   **WORTH THE WAIT**

PREP TIME: 10 minutes   **COOK SETTING:** High Pressure for 10 minutes   **RELEASE:** Natural for 10 minutes, then quick   **TOTAL TIME:** 45 minutes, plus 2 hours for chilling

This meal is made almost entirely from convenient pantry ingredients. I originally wrote the recipe as a hot entrée, but one of my testers found it also works great as a cold dish. Try it both ways to see which you prefer! **Serves 4 to 6**

1 cup millet

2 cups water, divided

2 medium tomatoes, diced

1 (14-ounce) can quartered artichoke hearts, drained

1 (6-ounce) jar pitted kalamata olives, drained

1 garlic clove, smashed

Zest and juice of 1 lemon

3 tablespoons tahini

2 teaspoons maple syrup

1 teaspoon no-salt-added Italian seasoning

Freshly ground black pepper

Salt (optional)

1. In your Instant Pot, combine the millet with 1¾ cups of the water. Lock the lid and turn the steam release handle to Sealing. Using the Pressure Cook/Manual function, set the cooker to High Pressure for 10 minutes.

2. In a large mixing bowl, stir together the tomatoes, artichokes, and olives and set aside. In a blender or food processor, make the dressing by combining the garlic, lemon zest and juice, tahini, maple syrup, and the remaining ¼ cup of water. Blend well.

3. When the cook time is complete, let the pressure release naturally for 10 minutes; quick-release any remaining pressure and carefully remove the lid. Fluff the millet with a fork and add it to the bowl of veggies. Add the dressing and Italian seasoning and season to taste with pepper and salt (if using). Toss to combine and chill at least 2 hours before serving. Store leftovers in the fridge for up to 4 days in a covered container.

FLAVOR BOOST: Turn this dish into a complete meal by adding a 15-ounce can of drained and rinsed chickpeas and a couple of handfuls of chopped baby spinach after cooking.

PER SERVING: Calories: 355; Fat: 12g; Protein: 11g; Total Carbs: 56g; Fiber: 14g; Sugar: 5g; Sodium: 378mg

"Refried" Beans

GLUTEN-FREE   NUT-FREE   SOY-FREE   WFPB   5 OR FEWER INGREDIENTS
WORTH THE WAIT

PREP TIME: 5 minutes   **COOK SETTING:** Sauté for 3 to 5 minutes, High Pressure for 45 minutes   **RELEASE:** Natural for 10 minutes, then quick   **TOTAL TIME:** 1 hour 10 minutes

Here's a surprise: "Refried" beans don't have to be fried at all! This recipe is for cooked, seasoned, and mashed pinto beans, but of course you could change things up and use black beans instead. There's no oil and no soaking, and most of the cooking time is hands-off!   Serves 4 to 6

1 **medium onion, diced**

3 **garlic cloves, crushed**

1 **teaspoon ground cumin**

7 **cups water**

1 **pound dried pinto beans (about 2 cups), rinsed and sorted**

1 **bay leaf**

Salt (optional)

LEFTOVERS TIP: Refried beans make a great base for a seven-layer dip. Top with the rice and lentil filling from the Southwestern Taco Bowls (page 80), sliced black olives, and Nut-Free Cheeze Sauce (page 113) and bake for 15 minutes at 350°F. Layer on Tofu Crema (see page 40), guacamole, lettuce, scallions, and diced tomatoes.

1. Select the Sauté function on your Instant Pot. Sauté the onion for 3 to 5 minutes, until translucent, adding water as needed to prevent sticking. Add the garlic and cumin and stir for 30 seconds, until fragrant. Cancel the Sauté function and add the water, beans, and bay leaf, scraping up any browned bits from the bottom of the pot. Lock the lid and turn the steam release handle to Sealing. Using the Pressure Cook/Manual function, set the cooker to High Pressure for 45 minutes.

2. When the cook time is complete, let the pressure release naturally for 10 minutes; quick-release any remaining pressure and carefully remove the lid. Remove and discard the bay leaf.

3. Drain the beans, saving 2 cups of the cooking liquid. Mash the beans using an immersion blender, adding the reserved cooking liquid as needed to achieve the desired texture. Add salt to taste (if using). Serve immediately. Store leftovers in the fridge for up to 4 days in a covered container.

PER SERVING: Calories: 410; Fat: 2g; Protein: 25g; Total Carbs: 74g; Fiber: 18g; Sugar: 4g; Sodium: 18mg

Forbidden Black Rice with Black Beans

GLUTEN-FREE   NUT-FREE   SOY-FREE   WFPB   5 OR FEWER INGREDIENTS
ONE-POT MEAL   WORTH THE WAIT

PREP TIME: 5 minutes   **COOK SETTING:** High Pressure for 30 minutes   **RELEASE:** Natural for 10 minutes, then quick   **TOTAL TIME:** 50 minutes

Called "forbidden rice" in China, black rice was often reserved exclusively for emperors, who savored its nutty and aromatic flavor. Today anyone can enjoy it, and this recipe with black beans makes a dramatic and delicious dish. **Serves 4 to 6**

4 cups water

1 cup black rice, rinsed

1 cup dried black beans, rinsed and sorted

½ cup diced onion

1 bay leaf

1 tablespoon maple syrup (optional)

1. In your Instant Pot, combine the water, rice, beans, onion, and bay leaf and stir well. Lock the lid and turn the steam release handle to Sealing. Using the Pressure Cook/Manual function, set the cooker to High Pressure for 30 minutes.

2. When the cook time is complete, let the pressure release naturally for 10 minutes; quick-release any remaining pressure and carefully remove the lid. Remove and discard the bay leaf. Stir in the maple syrup (if using). Serve immediately. Store any leftovers in the fridge for up to 4 days in a covered container.

FLAVOR BOOST: Try serving this dish with sliced avocado, chopped scallions, and a squeeze of lime.

PER SERVING: Calories: 342; Fat: 2g; Protein: 14g; Total Carbs: 67g; Fiber: 9g; Sugar: 2g; Sodium: 10mg

Cowboy Caviar

GLUTEN-FREE **NUT-FREE** **SOY-FREE** **WFPB** **WORTH THE WAIT**

PREP TIME: 10 minutes **COOK SETTING:** High Pressure for 17 minutes **RELEASE:** Natural for 10 minutes, then quick **TOTAL TIME:** 50 minutes

I owe this recipe to my wonderful mother-in-law, Anne. She introduced me to this flavor-packed dish several years ago, and I can't get enough of it as an appetizer served with our favorite scooping tortilla chips. Serves 4 to 6

1 pound dried black-eyed peas, rinsed and sorted

6½ cups water, plus 2 tablespoons

Zest and juice of 2 limes

2 tablespoons maple syrup

2 teaspoons gluten-free chili powder

1 cup frozen corn

2 bell peppers, diced

1 jalapeño pepper, diced (optional)

5 scallions, white and green parts, diced

3 tomatoes, diced

1 avocado, diced

½ bunch fresh cilantro, chopped

Freshly ground black pepper

Salt (optional)

1. In your Instant Pot, combine the peas and the 6½ cups of water. Lock the lid and turn the steam release handle to Sealing. Using the Pressure Cook/Manual function, set the cooker to High Pressure for 17 minutes.

2. In a large mixing bowl, whisk together the lime zest and juice, maple syrup, chili powder, and the remaining 2 tablespoons of water. Add the corn, bell peppers, jalapeño (if using), scallions, tomatoes, avocado, and cilantro and toss.

3. When the cook time is complete, let the pressure release naturally for 10 minutes; quick-release any remaining pressure and carefully remove the lid. Using a slotted spoon, remove the peas to a baking sheet and spread in a single layer to cool.

4. Add the cooled peas to the dressing and vegetables and gently toss. Season to taste with black pepper and salt (if using). Serve immediately. Store any leftovers in the fridge for up to 4 days in a covered container.

LEFTOVERS TIP: If making this dish ahead, wait to add the avocado until serving. Use leftovers to top a baked potato or as a salsa for a plant-based taco.

PER SERVING: Calories: 585; Fat: 10g; Protein: 29g; Total Carbs: 102g; Fiber: 26g; Sugar: 15g; Sodium: 63mg

Wild Rice and Farro Pilaf

SOY-FREE **WFPB** **WORTH THE WAIT**

PREP TIME: 5 minutes **COOK SETTING:** Sauté for 3 to 5 minutes, High Pressure for 25 minutes **RELEASE:** Natural for 5 minutes, then quick **TOTAL TIME:** 45 minutes

Pilaf is a popular restaurant dish because it looks as good as it tastes. With the sweetness from the raisins, the crunch from the almonds, and the pop of color and flavor from the parsley, this grain dish is just as great for company as it is for a weeknight side dish. **Serves 4 to 6**

½ medium onion, diced

2 garlic cloves, minced

½ teaspoon ground cinnamon

6 cups Easy Vegetable Broth (page 108) or no-salt-added vegetable broth

1½ cups pearled farro

¾ cup wild rice

¾ cup raisins

½ cup chopped almonds

3 tablespoons chopped parsley

Freshly ground black pepper

Salt (optional)

1. Select the Sauté function on your Instant Pot. Sauté the onion for 3 to 5 minutes, until translucent, adding water as needed to prevent sticking. Add the garlic and cinnamon and stir for 30 seconds, until fragrant.

2. Cancel the Sauté function and add the broth, farro, and rice. Stir well to combine, scraping any browned bits off the bottom of the pot. Lock the lid and turn the steam release handle to Sealing. Using the Pressure Cook/Manual function, set the cooker to High Pressure for 25 minutes.

3. When the cook time is complete, let the pressure release naturally for 5 minutes; quick-release any remaining pressure and carefully remove the lid. Stir in the raisins, almonds, and parsley and season to taste with pepper and salt (if using). Serve immediately. Store any leftovers in the fridge for up to 4 days in a covered container.

VARIATION TIP: To make this dish gluten-free, use brown rice or quinoa instead of farro.

PER SERVING: Calories: 529; Fat: 7g; Protein: 15g; Total Carbs: 107g; Fiber: 17g; Sugar: 19g; Sodium: 14mg

White Beans with Rosemary and Garlic

GLUTEN-FREE   NUT-FREE   SOY-FREE   WFPB   5 OR FEWER INGREDIENTS
WORTH THE WAIT

PREP TIME: 5 minutes   **COOK SETTING:** High Pressure for 32 minutes   **RELEASE:** Natural for 15 minutes, then quick   **TOTAL TIME:** 60 minutes

Beans are a nutritional powerhouse, providing fiber, protein, and many micronutrients, such as folate, magnesium, and vitamin B_6. Seasoned with a classic combination of rosemary and garlic, they are as delicious as they are good for you. **Serves 4 to 6**

2 cups water

1½ cups Easy Vegetable Broth (page 108) or no-salt-added vegetable broth

1 cup dried great northern beans, rinsed and sorted

4 garlic cloves, minced, divided

2 rosemary sprigs, or 2 teaspoons dried rosemary

Zest and juice of 1 lemon (optional)

Freshly ground black pepper

Salt (optional)

1. In your Instant Pot, combine the water, broth, beans, half the minced garlic, and rosemary. Lock the lid and turn the steam release handle to Sealing. Using the Pressure Cook/Manual function, set the cooker to High Pressure for 32 minutes.

2. When the cook time is complete, let the pressure release naturally for 15 minutes; quick-release any remaining pressure and carefully remove the lid. Remove and discard the rosemary stems. Using a slotted spoon, transfer the beans to a medium mixing bowl. Gently stir in the lemon zest and juice (if using) and the remaining garlic and season to taste with pepper and salt (if using). Serve immediately. Store any leftovers in the fridge for up to 4 days in a covered container.

VARIATION TIP: Chill and toss these flavorful beans with arugula, baby spinach, or other salad greens. Finish off the salad with a simple dressing of 3 tablespoons lemon juice or vinegar of choice, 2 tablespoons Dijon mustard, and 1 tablespoon maple syrup.

PER SERVING: Calories: 160; Fat: 1g; Protein: 10g; Total Carbs: 30g; Fiber: 9g; Sugar: 1g; Sodium: 7mg

Chickpea Salad Lettuce Wraps

GLUTEN-FREE **WORTH THE WAIT**

PREP TIME: 5 minutes **COOK SETTING:** High Pressure for 52 minutes
RELEASE: Natural **TOTAL TIME:** 1 hour 20 minutes

These wraps make a refreshing, crunchy, and tasty lunch. Adding poultry seasoning both before cooking the chickpeas and directly in the salad dressing gives this dish some familiar savory flavors. **Serves 4 to 6**

FOR THE TOFU MAYO

1 (8-ounce) package silken tofu

1 teaspoon freshly squeezed lemon juice

1 teaspoon white wine vinegar

½ teaspoon nutritional yeast

½ teaspoon mustard powder

¾ teaspoon salt

FOR THE CHICKPEAS

4 cups water

1 cup dried chickpeas, rinsed and sorted

¾ teaspoon no-salt-added poultry seasoning, divided

½ medium onion, roughly chopped

2 celery stalks, diced

¼ cup finely chopped onion

8 to 12 lettuce leaves, such as butter or romaine

Freshly ground black pepper

Salt (optional)

1. **To make the tofu mayo:** In a blender or food processor, combine the tofu, lemon juice, vinegar, nutritional yeast, mustard, and salt. Blend well and refrigerate until needed.

2. **To cook the chickpeas:** In your Instant Pot, combine the water, chickpeas, ¼ teaspoon of the poultry seasoning, and the roughly chopped onion. Lock the lid and turn the steam release handle to Sealing. Set the cooker to High Pressure for 52 minutes.

3. When the cook time is complete, let the pressure release naturally. Remove the chickpeas to a large mixing bowl and let cool.

4. Mash the cooled chickpeas with a fork or potato masher, leaving most beans partially intact. Add the finely chopped onion, celery, the remaining ½ teaspoon of poultry seasoning, and ½ cup of the tofu mayo. Stir well to combine. Season to taste with pepper and salt (if using). Portion about ¼ cup onto each lettuce leaf. Roll and serve immediately. Refrigerate leftover tofu mayo for up to 10 days and salad for up to 3 days.

VARIATION TIP: Turn this it into a sandwich and layer it with sliced radishes and sprouts or microgreens.

PER SERVING: Calories: 242; Fat: 5g; Protein: 15g; Total Carbs: 36g; Fiber: 7g; Sugar: 7g; Sodium: 469mg

Farro Risotto

NUT-FREE **SOY-FREE** **WFPB** **5 OR FEWER INGREDIENTS** **WORTH THE WAIT**

PREP TIME: 5 minutes **COOK SETTING:** Sauté for 3 to 5 minutes, High Pressure for 10 minutes **RELEASE:** Natural for 10 minutes, then quick **TOTAL TIME:** 45 minutes

Risotto is an Italian dish traditionally made with rice, but other grains can be substituted. Here, we use heartier farro. Add ½ cup of plant-based parmesan plus ¼ cup of white wine when pouring in the broth for even more flavor. **Serves 4 to 6**

1 medium onion, diced

4 garlic cloves, minced

1½ cups Easy Vegetable Broth (page 108) or no-salt-added vegetable broth

1 cup pearled farro

2 thyme sprigs, or 1 teaspoon dried thyme

Freshly ground black pepper

Salt (optional)

1. Select the Sauté function on your Instant Pot. Sauté the onion for 3 to 5 minutes, until translucent, adding water as needed to prevent sticking. Add the garlic and stir for 30 seconds, until fragrant.

2. Cancel the Sauté function and add the broth, farro, and thyme. Stir well to combine, scraping any browned bits off the bottom. Lock the lid and turn the steam release handle to Sealing. Using the Pressure Cook/Manual function, set the cooker to High Pressure for 10 minutes.

3. When the cook time is complete, let the pressure release naturally for 10 minutes; quick-release any remaining pressure and carefully remove the lid. Remove the thyme stems.

4. Season to taste with pepper and salt (if using). Serve immediately. Store any leftovers in the fridge for up to 4 days in a covered container.

VARIATION TIP: Make this into a one-pot meal by sautéing 8 ounces of sliced mushrooms with the onions. After removing the lid, stir in 3 to 5 ounces of fresh baby spinach until wilted.

PER SERVING: Calories: 192; Fat: 1g; Protein: 5g; Total Carbs: 42g; Fiber: 8g; Sugar: 2g; Sodium: 6mg

Kansas City–Style Barbecue Beans

GLUTEN-FREE   NUT-FREE   SOY-FREE   WFPB   WORTH THE WAIT

PREP TIME: 5 minutes   **COOK SETTING:** Sauté for 3 to 5 minutes, High Pressure for 1 hour 15 minutes   **RELEASE:** Natural for 15 to 20 minutes   **TOTAL TIME:** 1 hour 40 minutes

Thanks to the Instant Pot, my beans come out perfect every time, and this recipe is my secret for the best-ever barbecue beans. Adding salt to the dried beans can prevent them from softening, so be sure to save it (if using) for the end. **Serves 4 to 6**

1 medium onion, diced

1 (6-ounce) can
   tomato paste

3 garlic cloves, crushed

2 teaspoons
   smoked paprika

2 cups water

2 cups Easy Vegetable
   Broth (page 108)
   or no-salt-added
   vegetable broth

⅓ cup maple syrup

¼ cup apple cider vinegar

2 tablespoons
   stone-ground mustard

1 pound dried navy beans
   (about 2 cups), rinsed
   and sorted

2 bay leaves

Salt (optional)

1. Select the Sauté function on your Instant Pot. Sauté the onion for 3 to 5 minutes, until translucent, adding water as needed to prevent sticking. Add the tomato paste, garlic, and paprika and stir for 30 seconds, until fragrant. Stir in the water, broth, maple syrup, vinegar, and mustard, scraping up any browned bits from the bottom of the pot. Stir in the beans and bay leaves. Lock the lid and turn the steam release handle to Sealing. Using the Pressure Cook/Manual function, set the cooker to High Pressure for 1 hour 15 minutes.

2. When the cook time is complete, let the pressure release naturally (15 to 20 minutes) and carefully remove the lid. Remove and discard the bay leaves. Stir, season to taste with salt (if using), and serve immediately. Store any leftovers in the fridge for up to 4 days in a covered container.

VARIATION TIP: My buddy Brian Rodgers, award-winning chef and former Kansas City pitmaster, stirs 1 cup of raisins, 1 chopped apple, and a tablespoon of sesame oil into his pit beans at the end. Give it a try!

PER SERVING: Calories: 521; Fat: 3g; Protein: 29g; Total Carbs: 99g; Fiber: 20g; Sugar: 27g; Sodium: 37mg

Red Lentil Dal with Kale

GLUTEN-FREE **SOY-FREE** **WFPB** **ONE-POT MEAL**

PREP TIME: 10 minutes **COOK SETTING:** Sauté for 3 to 5 minutes, High Pressure for 7 minutes **RELEASE:** Natural for 10 minutes, then quick **TOTAL TIME:** 40 minutes

Red lentils are faster-cooking and creamier than both the green and brown varieties. This Indian-inspired dish can be served as a one-pot meal on its own or over rice. **Serves 4 to 6**

1 large onion, diced

4 garlic cloves, minced

1 (1-inch) knob fresh ginger, peeled and grated

1 tablespoon garam masala

¼ teaspoon red pepper flakes (optional)

3 cups water

1½ cups dry red lentils, rinsed and sorted

1 large carrot, diced

1 Roma tomato, diced

3 or 4 fresh kale leaves, stemmed and chopped

1 (14-ounce) can full-fat coconut milk

Zest and juice of 1 lemon

Freshly ground black pepper

Salt (optional)

Fresh cilantro (optional)

1. Select the Sauté function on your Instant Pot. Sauté the onion for 3 to 5 minutes, until translucent, adding water as needed to prevent sticking. Add the garlic, ginger, garam masala, and red pepper flakes (if using) and stir for 30 seconds, until fragrant.

2. Cancel the Sauté function and add the water, lentils, carrot, and tomato and stir well to combine. Place the kale on top. Lock the lid and turn the steam release handle to Sealing. Using the Pressure Cook/Manual function, set the cooker to High Pressure for 7 minutes.

3. When the cook time is complete, let the pressure release naturally for 10 minutes; quick-release any remaining pressure and carefully remove the lid. Stir in the coconut milk and lemon zest and juice, then season to taste with pepper and salt (if using). Serve immediately, topped with cilantro (if using). Store leftovers in the fridge for up to 4 days in a covered container.

FLAVOR BOOST: Create your own spice blend in place of the garam masala by combining equal amounts of ground mustard seed, ground cumin, ground turmeric, curry powder, paprika, ground cinnamon, and ground coriander.

PER SERVING: Calories: 495; Fat: 23g; Protein: 21g; Total Carbs: 58g; Fiber: 10g; Sugar: 4g; Sodium: 36mg

Jackfruit Sloppy Joes, page 85

CHAPTER 6
Entrées

Southwestern Taco Bowls

`GLUTEN-FREE` `NUT-FREE` `SOY-FREE` `WFPB` `ONE-POT MEAL` `QUICK`

PREP TIME: 5 minutes **COOK SETTING:** High Pressure for 16 minutes **RELEASE:** Quick
TOTAL TIME: 30 minutes

Everyone needs a quick and easy go-to taco filling recipe, and this is it! While the filling cooks in the Instant Pot, prepare the salad portion of the meal. Or serve these as tacos using your favorite tortillas with "Refried" Beans (page 68), Tofu Crema (see page 40), and any other toppings you love. **Serves 4 to 6**

4 cups Easy Vegetable Broth (page 108) or no-salt-added vegetable broth

2 cups long-grain brown rice

2 cups green or brown lentils, rinsed and sorted

½ cup salsa

2 teaspoons fennel seeds

1 tablespoon gluten-free chili powder

2 teaspoons onion powder

Juice of 4 limes, divided

Salt (optional)

8 to 12 cups shredded lettuce

2 avocados, diced

1. In your Instant Pot, stir together the broth, rice, lentils, salsa, fennel, chili powder, and onion powder. Lock the lid and turn the steam release handle to Sealing. Using the Pressure Cook/Manual function, set the cooker to High Pressure for 16 minutes.

2. When the cook time is complete, quick-release the pressure and carefully remove the lid. Add half the lime juice and salt to taste (if using). Fluff with a fork to combine.

3. Toss the lettuce with the remaining lime juice. For serving, add about 2 cups of the lettuce to each plate, top with the rice and lentils, and garnish with the diced avocado.

LEFTOVERS TIP: Create enchiladas by mixing the taco filling with some Cauliflower Queso (page 32). Spread "Refried" Beans (page 68) on a tortilla and top with the filling. Roll and place in a casserole dish. Cover with enchilada sauce and bake for 15 minutes at 350°F.

PER SERVING: Calories: 892; Fat: 19g; Protein: 36g; Total Carbs: 152g; Fiber: 24g; Sugar: 7g; Sodium: 315mg

Potato Salad with Mixed Greens and Mustard Dressing

GLUTEN-FREE **NUT-FREE** **SOY-FREE** **WFPB** **QUICK**

PREP TIME: 10 minutes **COOK SETTING:** High Pressure for 4 minutes **RELEASE:** Natural for 5 minutes, then quick **TOTAL TIME:** 30 minutes

This French-inspired salad comes together in a snap. Whisk together the dressing while the potatoes cook, and the hot potatoes will absorb all the fabulous flavors when you pour it over them. *Serves 4 to 6*

1 cup water

2 tablespoons apple cider vinegar, divided

2 pounds baby red potatoes, cut into 1-inch chunks

1 garlic clove, minced

3 tablespoons red wine vinegar

3 tablespoons stone-ground mustard

1 tablespoon maple syrup

2 teaspoons herbes de Provence

Freshly ground black pepper

Salt (optional)

16 ounces mixed salad greens

1 cup diced scallions, white and green parts

2 tablespoons chopped fresh dill or flat-leaf parsley

1. In your Instant Pot, combine the water and 1 tablespoon of the cider vinegar. Place the potatoes in a steamer basket inside the pot. Lock and seal the lid. Set the cooker to High Pressure for 4 minutes.

2. In a medium bowl, whisk together the remaining 1 tablespoon of cider vinegar, the garlic, wine vinegar, mustard, maple syrup, and herbes de Provence and season to taste with pepper and salt (if using). Set aside.

3. When the cook time is complete, release pressure naturally for 5 minutes; quick-release any remaining pressure and carefully remove the lid. Transfer the potatoes to a large bowl. Add half the dressing and toss to coat.

4. In a large bowl, combine the greens and scallions, pour the remaining dressing over them, and toss to coat. Serve the potatoes on the greens, garnished with dill or parsley.

INGREDIENT TIP: Baby potatoes of any kind work in this recipe, as do larger red or yellow potatoes. Cutting them uniformly into 1-inch chunks allows them to cook fully in the same amount of time.

PER SERVING: Calories: 207; Fat: 1g; Protein: 7g; Total Carbs: 45g; Fiber: 6g; Sugar: 8g; Sodium: 182mg

Sesame Chickpeas and Veggies

GLUTEN-FREE WFPB ONE-POT MEAL QUICK

PREP TIME: 5 minutes **COOK SETTING:** Sauté for 5 to 7 minutes **RELEASE:** None
TOTAL TIME: 20 minutes

My family loves a take-out dish smothered in a sweet and sticky sauce. Here, we stir-fry chickpeas at home with a bag of precut frozen veggies for a quick and easy meal. If you like, you can chop up your favorite fresh veggies in place of the prepackaged kind. **Serves 4 to 6**

3 tablespoons arrowroot powder or cornstarch

½ cup tamari, coconut aminos, or low-sodium gluten-free soy sauce

3 tablespoons maple syrup

1 tablespoon rice vinegar

1⅓ cups Easy Vegetable Broth (page 108) or no-salt-added vegetable broth, divided

2 tablespoons toasted sesame oil (optional)

1 (12-ounce) bag frozen stir-fry vegetables

2 teaspoons garlic powder

2 teaspoons ground ginger

1 (15-ounce) can chickpeas, drained and rinsed

Hot cooked rice, for serving (optional)

2 tablespoons toasted sesame seeds

3 scallions, white and green parts, diced (optional)

1. In a medium bowl, whisk together the arrowroot, tamari, maple syrup, vinegar, and 1 cup of the broth. Set aside.

2. Select the Sauté function on your Instant Pot and heat the oil (if using). Sauté the vegetables, adding 2 to 4 tablespoons of the broth as needed to prevent sticking, until they are heated through, 5 to 7 minutes. Stir in the garlic and ginger.

3. When the vegetables are cooked, remove them to a large bowl. Add the tamari mixture and chickpeas to the pot. Stir until boiling and thickened. Return the vegetables to the pot and toss to combine. Serve over hot cooked rice (if using) with sesame seeds and scallions (if using) on top.

VARIATION TIP: Have a bit more time? Use your Instant Pot to cook 1 cup of dried chickpeas with 4 cups of water seasoned with a teaspoon each of garlic powder and ground ginger for 52 minutes on High Pressure with a natural release. Or instead of the chickpeas, try this dish with a plant-based frozen chick'n substitute, such as Quorn brand, and sauté it with the vegetables.

PER SERVING: Calories: 274; Fat: 4g; Protein: 12g; Total Carbs: 48g; Fiber: 9g; Sugar: 12g; Sodium: 923mg

Veggie Lo Mein

WFPB **ONE-POT MEAL** **QUICK**

PREP TIME: 10 minutes **COOK SETTING:** Sauté for 3 to 5 minutes, High Pressure for 5 minutes **RELEASE:** Natural for 5 minutes, then quick **TOTAL TIME:** 30 minutes

In this one-pot meal, we cook most of the veggies first so they stay crisp. To avoid the Instant Pot burn message, be sure to place the cabbage under the noodles so they don't stick to the bottom of the pot. **Serves 4 to 6**

1 tablespoon water or sesame oil

2 (10- to 12-ounce) packages frozen stir-fry vegetables

3 cups Easy Vegetable Broth (page 108) or no-salt-added vegetable broth

¼ cup coconut aminos, tamari, or low-sodium gluten-free soy sauce

2 tablespoons rice vinegar

2 tablespoons maple syrup

3 garlic cloves, minced

2 teaspoons ground ginger

¼ to ½ teaspoon red pepper flakes (optional)

½ head napa cabbage, chopped

12 ounces whole wheat spaghetti

Freshly ground black pepper

Salt (optional)

1. Select the Sauté function on your Instant Pot and heat the water or oil. Sauté the vegetables for 3 to 5 minutes, until crisp-tender. Remove from the pot and set aside.

2. Turn off the Sauté function. In the pot, whisk together the broth, coconut aminos, rice vinegar, maple syrup, garlic, ginger, and red pepper flakes (if using). Place the cabbage on top of the sauce but do not stir. Break the spaghetti in half and place it on top of the cabbage.

3. Lock the lid and turn the steam release handle to Sealing. Using the Pressure Cook/Manual function, set the cooker to High Pressure for 5 minutes.

4. When the cook time is complete, let the pressure release naturally for 5 minutes; quick-release any remaining pressure and carefully remove the lid. Return the veggies to the pot and stir until well combined. Season to taste with pepper and salt (if using). Serve immediately. Store any leftovers in the fridge for up to 4 days in a covered container.

VARIATION TIP: You can purchase all sorts of frozen veggies that may or may not be included in a premade mix. Just keep the measurements about the same.

PER SERVING: Calories: 463; Fat: 2g; Protein: 20g; Total Carbs: 97g; Fiber: 15g; Sugar: 9g; Sodium: 660mg

Butternut Squash Mac and Cheeze

SOY-FREE **WFPB** **QUICK**

PREP TIME: 10 minutes **COOK SETTING:** High Pressure for 4 minutes **RELEASE:** Quick
TOTAL TIME: 30 minutes

If you love a rich, creamy, and comforting mac and cheese, this is the perfect plant-based recipe for you. To make this dish gluten-free, simply use your favorite gluten-free noodles. **Serves 4 to 6**

3 cups water

1 cup peeled and diced butternut squash (fresh or frozen)

1 cup diced yellow potatoes

½ cup raw cashews

⅓ cup diced onion

3 tablespoons nutritional yeast

2 tablespoons chickpea miso paste

1 tablespoon freshly squeezed lemon juice

½ teaspoon paprika

Freshly ground black pepper

Salt (optional)

1 pound hot cooked elbow noodles

1. In your Instant Pot, combine the water, squash, potatoes, cashews, and onion. Lock the lid and turn the steam release handle to Sealing. Using the Pressure Cook/Manual function, set the cooker to High Pressure for 4 minutes.

2. In a blender, combine the nutritional yeast, miso, lemon juice, and paprika. When the cook time is complete, quick-release the pressure and carefully remove the lid. Using a slotted spoon, remove the cashews and vegetables to the blender, along with 1 cup of the cooking liquid. Blend until smooth and creamy. Season to taste with pepper and salt (if using).

3. Place the elbow noodles in a large casserole dish and stir in the sauce. Serve immediately.

FLAVOR BOOST: Make a crispy topping by mixing ⅓ cup of panko bread crumbs and 2 tablespoons of melted plant-based butter in a small bowl. Sprinkle evenly over the top of the casserole dish before serving, and place under the broiler for about 1 minute, until the topping is golden brown.

PER SERVING: Calories: 344; Fat: 9g; Protein: 12g; Total Carbs: 55g; Fiber: 5g; Sugar: 4g; Sodium: 325mg

Jackfruit Sloppy Joes

GLUTEN-FREE **NUT-FREE** **SOY-FREE** **WFPB** **QUICK**

PREP TIME: 5 minutes **COOK SETTING:** High Pressure for 5 minutes **RELEASE:** Natural for 10 minutes, then quick **TOTAL TIME:** 30 minutes

For a simple meal, enjoy these tangy, sweet, and satisfying sandwiches any day of the week. I serve mine with Kansas City–Style Barbecue Beans (page 75) and Butternut Squash Mac and Cheeze (page 84) topped with a little steamed broccoli for a full meal. *Serves 4 to 6*

2 (20-ounce) cans young green jackfruit, drained

1 cup Easy Vegetable Broth (page 108) or no-salt-added vegetable broth

½ medium onion, diced

½ green bell pepper, diced

¼ cup no-salt-added tomato sauce

2 garlic cloves, minced

1 tablespoon gluten-free vegan Worcestershire sauce

1 tablespoon maple syrup

1 teaspoon ground cumin

Freshly ground black pepper

Salt (optional)

8 to 12 gluten-free hamburger buns

1. In your Instant Pot, break up the jackfruit using a potato masher or two forks. Add the broth, onion, bell pepper, tomato sauce, garlic, Worcestershire sauce, maple syrup, and cumin. Season to taste with black pepper and salt (if using) and stir to combine. Lock the lid and turn the steam release handle to Sealing. Using the Pressure Cook/ Manual function, set the cooker to High Pressure for 5 minutes.

2. When the cook time is complete, let the pressure release naturally for 10 minutes; quick-release any remaining pressure and carefully remove the lid. Stir and break up any remaining large pieces of jackfruit. Adjust the seasoning to taste.

3. Lightly toast the buns in the oven. Serve a heaping ¼ cup of the sloppy joe mixture on each bun. Store any filling leftovers in the fridge for up to 4 days in a covered container.

VARIATION TIP: For a higher protein meal, substitute two 15-ounce cans of lentils for the jackfruit, or use one 15-ounce can of lentils and one 20-ounce can of jackfruit.

PER SERVING: Calories: 509; Fat: 5g; Protein: 13g; Total Carbs: 109g; Fiber: 6g; Sugar: 59g; Sodium: 471mg

Tofu Tikka Masala

GLUTEN-FREE **WFPB** **WORTH THE WAIT**

PREP TIME: 30 minutes **COOK SETTING:** Sauté for 8 minutes, High Pressure for 10 minutes, then quick **RELEASE:** Natural for 10 minutes **TOTAL TIME:** 1 hour

For this Indian-inspired dish, I let the tofu marinate to take on the flavors in the spiced sauce before cooking. This recipe makes plenty of sauce for serving over rice or for dipping warm pieces of naan into. Serves 4 to 6

1 medium onion, diced, divided

¼ cup water

6 garlic cloves, crushed

1 (1-inch) knob ginger, peeled and grated

1 tablespoon gluten-free chili powder

1 tablespoon garam masala

1 teaspoon ground turmeric

1 (14-ounce) package extra-firm tofu, pressed and cubed

½ medium green bell pepper, diced

1 (15-ounce) can diced no-salt-added tomatoes

1 (14-ounce) can full-fat coconut milk

Hot cooked rice, for serving (optional)

Small bunch cilantro, chopped (optional)

1. In a blender, combine half the onion with the water, garlic, ginger, chili powder, garam masala, and turmeric and blend well. In a medium bowl, gently toss the tofu with the sauce.

2. Select the Sauté function on your Instant Pot. Sauté the remaining onion and bell pepper for 5 minutes, adding water as needed to prevent sticking. Add the tofu mixture and sauté for 3 minutes. Add the tomatoes, turn off the Sauté function, and stir well.

3. Lock the lid and turn the steam release handle to Sealing. Using the Pressure Cook/Manual function, set the cooker to High Pressure for 10 minutes.

4. When the cook time is complete, let the pressure release naturally for 10 minutes; quick-release any remaining pressure and carefully remove the lid. Stir in the coconut milk, ¼ cup at a time, for the desired consistency. Serve over hot cooked rice (if using) and garnish with cilantro (if using).

INGREDIENT TIP: You'll need to press your tofu to remove excess liquid. Wrap it in paper towels and press with a heavy skillet for about 30 minutes.

PER SERVING: Calories: 331; Fat: 27g; Protein: 14g; Total Carbs: 15g; Fiber: 4g; Sugar: 5g; Sodium: 91mg

Portobello Pot Roast

GLUTEN-FREE **NUT-FREE** **SOY-FREE** **WFPB**

PREP TIME: 10 minutes **COOK SETTING:** Sauté for 9 to 11 minutes, High Pressure for 15 minutes **RELEASE:** Quick **TOTAL TIME:** 35 minutes

If you're looking for classic pot roast flavors, the rich meatiness of portobello mushrooms will not disappoint. The gravy in this recipe deserves a nice hunk of crusty bread to soak up every last drop. **Serves 4 to 6**

1 medium onion, diced

1 pound portobello mushrooms (about 5), gills removed, sliced into large pieces

5 medium yellow potatoes, cut into 2-inch pieces

4 medium carrots, cut into 2-inch pieces

2 cups Easy Vegetable Broth (page 108) or no-salt-added vegetable broth

1½ cups red wine, Easy Vegetable Broth (page 108), or no-salt-added vegetable broth

3 tablespoons tomato paste

3 tablespoons gluten-free vegan Worcestershire sauce

2 thyme sprigs, or 1 teaspoon dried thyme

⅓ cup water

3 tablespoons arrowroot powder

Freshly ground black pepper

Salt (optional)

1. Select the Sauté function on your Instant Pot. Sauté the onion for 3 minutes, adding water as needed to prevent sticking. Add the mushrooms and sauté until lightly golden, about 4 minutes. Stir in the potatoes, carrots, broth, wine, tomato paste, Worcestershire sauce, and thyme, stirring well and scraping up any browned bits from the bottom of the pot. Cancel the Sauté function.

2. Lock the lid and turn the steam release handle to Sealing. Using the Pressure Cook/Manual function, set the cooker to High Pressure for 15 minutes.

3. When the cook time is complete, quick-release the pressure and carefully remove the lid. Discard the thyme stems. In a small bowl, whisk together the water and arrowroot. Select the Sauté function and add the arrowroot slurry, stirring until thickened, 2 to 4 minutes. Season to taste with pepper and salt (if using). Serve immediately. Store any leftovers in the fridge for up to 4 days in a covered container.

INGREDIENT TIP: Portobello mushrooms have large, dense caps with black gills underneath. To remove the gills, scrape them off gently with a spoon.

PER SERVING: Calories: 307; Fat: 1g; Protein: 9g; Total Carbs: 69g; Fiber: 10g; Sugar: 12g; Sodium: 202mg

Zucchini, Kale, and Mushroom Pasta Marinara

NUT-FREE   SOY-FREE   WFPB   ONE-POT MEAL

PREP TIME: 10 minutes   **COOK SETTING:** Sauté for 8 minutes, High Pressure for 7 minutes   **RELEASE:** Quick   **TOTAL TIME:** 40 minutes

The secret to cooking pasta in the Instant Pot is to have the right ratio of water to pasta, not to overfill the pot, and to keep the pasta away from the bottom to avoid burning. Here, I layer plenty of veggies below the pasta so it cooks perfectly.   **Serves 4 to 6**

1 medium onion, diced

8 ounces white button or cremini mushrooms

4 garlic cloves, minced

3 tablespoons tomato paste

1 tablespoon no-salt-added Italian seasoning

3 cups water

2 (15-ounce) cans no-salt-added diced tomatoes

2 tablespoons balsamic vinegar

1 bunch Tuscan kale, stemmed and chopped

12 ounces whole wheat penne or other short pasta

1 medium zucchini, cut into 1-inch pieces

Freshly ground black pepper

Salt (optional)

1. Select the Sauté function on your Instant Pot. Sauté the onion for 3 minutes, adding water as needed to prevent sticking. Add the mushrooms and sauté for 5 minutes. Add the garlic, tomato paste, and Italian seasoning and stir for 30 seconds, until fragrant. Cancel the Sauté function. Stir in the water, tomatoes, and vinegar. Layer the kale, then the pasta, and finally the zucchini on top but do not stir. Lock the lid and turn the steam release handle to Sealing. Using the Pressure Cook/Manual function, set the cooker to High Pressure for 7 minutes.

2. When the cook time is complete, quick-release the pressure and carefully remove the lid. Stir and season to taste with pepper and salt (if using). Serve immediately. Store any leftovers in the fridge for up to 4 days in a covered container.

INGREDIENT TIP: Tuscan kale, also known as dinosaur kale or lacinato kale, is a darker green than curly kale with waxy, bumpy leaves. You can use curly kale in this recipe instead if you prefer.

PER SERVING: Calories: 391; Fat: 2g; Protein: 18g; Total Carbs: 83g; Fiber: 13g; Sugar: 12g; Sodium: 51mg

Yellow Split Pea and Broccoli Curry

GLUTEN-FREE NUT-FREE SOY-FREE WFPB ONE-POT MEAL QUICK

PREP TIME: 10 minutes **COOK SETTING:** Sauté for 3 minutes, High Pressure for 5 minutes **RELEASE:** Natural for 5 minutes, then quick **TOTAL TIME:** 30 minutes

Broccoli florets are delicious but delicate. The secret to not overcooking them is to add them after pressure-cooking and allow the residual heat to steam the broccoli to the ideal crisp-tender texture. **Serves 4 to 6**

1 medium onion, diced

3 garlic cloves, minced

1 (1-inch) knob ginger, peeled and grated

2 teaspoons curry powder

½ teaspoon red pepper flakes (optional)

2½ cups water

1 (15-ounce) can diced no-salt-added tomatoes

1 cup yellow split peas, rinsed and sorted

2 heads broccoli florets, chopped into bite-size pieces

Zest and juice of 2 limes

Freshly ground black pepper

Salt (optional)

Hot cooked rice, for serving (optional)

1. Select the Sauté function on your Instant Pot. Sauté the onion for 3 minutes, adding water as needed to prevent sticking. Add the garlic, ginger, curry powder, and red pepper flakes (if using) and stir for 30 seconds, until fragrant. Turn off the Sauté function and stir in the water, tomatoes, and split peas.

2. Lock the lid and turn the steam release handle to Sealing. Using the Pressure Cook/Manual function, set the cooker to High Pressure for 5 minutes.

3. When the cook time is complete, let the pressure release naturally for 5 minutes; quick-release any remaining pressure and carefully remove the lid. Stir in the broccoli, close the lid, and let steam for 5 minutes. Stir in the lime zest and juice and season to taste with pepper and salt (if using). Serve immediately over hot cooked rice (if using).

INGREDIENT TIP: Yellow split peas are earthier than the green variety. I love the color and flavor contrast between the yellow peas and the broccoli, but you can use green peas if you prefer.

PER SERVING: Calories: 317; Fat: 2g; Protein: 22g; Total Carbs: 61g; Fiber: 24g; Sugar: 13g; Sodium: 121mg

Three-Mushroom Stroganoff

SOY-FREE   WFPB   QUICK

PREP TIME: 10 minutes **COOK SETTING:** Sauté for 7 to 11 minutes, High Pressure for 4 minutes **RELEASE:** Quick **TOTAL TIME:** 30 minutes

Using a combination of mushrooms gives this stroganoff a variety of meaty bites in a tangy, creamy sauce. This family favorite is comforting enough for any day of the week, and if you serve it in a fancy bowl, it's delicious enough for company. **Serves 4 to 6**

1 medium onion, diced

24 ounces white button, cremini, and shiitake mushrooms

1 (6-ounce) can tomato paste

2 teaspoons dried thyme

4 cups Easy Vegetable Broth (page 108) or no-salt-added vegetable broth

2 tablespoons gluten-free vegan Worcestershire sauce

2 tablespoons arrowroot powder

½ cup water

½ cup raw cashews, soaked in hot water for 15 minutes, then drained

½ cup no-salt-added canned or home-cooked white beans, drained and rinsed

Freshly ground black pepper

Salt (optional)

1 pound hot cooked pasta, for serving

1. Select the Sauté function on your Instant Pot. Sauté the onion for 3 minutes, adding water as needed to prevent sticking. Add the mushrooms and sauté for 2 to 4 minutes, until they release their liquid. Stir in the tomato paste and thyme. Turn off the Sauté function and stir in the broth and Worcestershire sauce.

2. Lock the lid and turn the steam release handle to Sealing. Using the Pressure Cook/Manual function, set the cooker to High Pressure for 4 minutes.

3. In a small bowl, whisk together the arrowroot and ¼ cup of the water. Set aside. In a blender, blend the cashews, beans, and the remaining ¼ cup of water.

4. When the cook time is complete, quick-release the pressure and carefully remove the lid. Select the Sauté function and stir in the arrowroot slurry until thickened, 2 to 4 minutes. Stir in the cashew cream and season to taste with pepper and salt (if using). Serve immediately over hot pasta.

LEFTOVER TIP: Serve over a baked potato for a hearty and delicious lunch.

PER SERVING: Calories: 373; Fat: 9g; Protein: 19g; Total Carbs: 62g; Fiber: 11g; Sugar: 13g; Sodium: 125mg

Potato and Kale Curry

GLUTEN-FREE SOY-FREE WFPB ONE-POT MEAL QUICK

PREP TIME: 10 minutes **COOK SETTING:** Sauté for 5 to 7 minutes, High Pressure for 6 minutes **RELEASE:** Natural for 5 minutes, then quick **TOTAL TIME:** 30 minutes

Hearty and simple, this tasty curry is a fast and easy meal. The starch from the potatoes creates a delicious, thick stew-like sauce. **Serves 4 to 6**

1 medium onion, diced

4 garlic cloves, minced

2 tablespoons curry powder

½ teaspoon red pepper flakes (optional)

2¼ cups water, divided

1 (14-ounce) can full-fat coconut milk

2 pounds red or yellow potatoes, cut into 1-inch pieces

1 tablespoon maple syrup (optional)

1 bunch Tuscan kale, stemmed

1 (15-ounce) can chickpeas, drained and rinsed

3 tablespoons arrowroot powder

Freshly ground black pepper

Salt (optional)

1. Select the Sauté function on your Instant Pot. Sauté the onion for 3 minutes, adding water as needed to prevent sticking. Add the garlic, curry powder, and red pepper flakes (if using) and stir for 30 seconds, until fragrant. Turn off the Sauté function and stir in 2 cups of the water, the coconut milk, potatoes, and maple syrup (if using). Place the kale on top.

2. Lock the lid and turn the steam release handle to Sealing. Using the Pressure Cook/Manual function, set the cooker to High Pressure for 6 minutes.

3. When the cook time is complete, let the pressure release naturally for 5 minutes; quick-release any remaining pressure and carefully remove the lid. Stir in the chickpeas. In a small bowl, whisk together the arrowroot and the remaining ¼ cup of water. Select the Sauté function and stir in the arrowroot slurry until thickened, 2 to 4 minutes. Season to taste with pepper and salt (if using).

INGREDIENT TIP: If you don't have curry powder, make your own blend with 1 tablespoon ground turmeric and ½ teaspoon each of garlic powder, onion powder, ground coriander, ground cumin, and mustard powder.

PER SERVING: Calories: 523; Fat: 24g; Protein: 13g; Total Carbs: 71g; Fiber: 12g; Sugar: 11g; Sodium: 68mg

Creamy Spaghetti Squash with Spinach, Olives, and Roasted Red Peppers

GLUTEN-FREE **WFPB** QUICK

PREP TIME: 10 minutes **COOK SETTING:** High Pressure for 8 minutes **RELEASE:** Quick
TOTAL TIME: 30 minutes

Using pantry ingredients like kalamata olives and jarred roasted red peppers makes this dish both easy and flavorful. You can even whip up the quick sauce in the blender while the squash cooks. **Serves 4 to 6**

1 cup water

1 (2- to 4-pound) spaghetti squash, halved and seeded

¾ cup unsweetened plant-based milk

1 cup no-salt-added canned white beans, drained and rinsed

2 garlic cloves, smashed

2 tablespoons nutritional yeast

Zest and juice of 1 lemon

Freshly ground black pepper

Salt (optional)

5 ounces fresh baby spinach

1 (6-ounce) jar pitted kalamata olives, drained and chopped

2 or 3 jarred roasted red peppers, chopped

¼ cup chopped flat-leaf parsley

1. Pour the water into your Instant Pot and insert the trivet. Place the squash on the trivet. Lock the lid and turn the steam release handle to Sealing. Using the Pressure Cook/Manual function, set the cooker to High Pressure for 8 minutes.

2. In a blender or food processor, combine the milk, beans, garlic, nutritional yeast, and lemon zest and juice and season to taste with black pepper and salt (if using). Blend well. Set aside.

3. When the cook time is complete, quick-release the pressure and carefully remove the lid. Drain the squash. Using a fork, remove the pulp of the squash, shredding it into long spaghetti-like strands. Discard the skin. Add the spinach, olives, red peppers, and sauce and toss to combine. Stir in half the parsley and serve immediately, garnished with the remaining parsley.

INGREDIENT TIP: Spaghetti squash is unique for its ability to shred into what looks like long strands of spaghetti noodles. Look for a squash that is firm, be careful when cutting it in half, and use a very sharp knife.

PER SERVING: Calories: 206; Fat: 5g; Protein: 9g; Total Carbs: 36g; Fiber: 9g; Sugar: 10g; Sodium: 363mg

Turmeric-Spiced Cabbage, Potatoes, and Carrots

GLUTEN-FREE NUT-FREE SOY-FREE WFPB ONE-POT MEAL QUICK

PREP TIME: 10 minutes **COOK SETTING:** Sauté for 3 minutes, High Pressure for 2 minutes **RELEASE:** Quick **TOTAL TIME:** 25 minutes

If you're looking for a quick and easy weeknight meal, this is it, especially if you use pre-shredded cabbage and bagged baby carrots. This recipe is inspired by an Ethiopian dish, but see the Variation Tip below for alternatives to this simple one-pot meal. *Serves 4 to 6*

1 medium onion, diced

1 (1-inch) knob ginger, peeled and grated

1 teaspoon paprika

1 teaspoon ground cumin

½ teaspoon ground turmeric

3 medium yellow potatoes, cut into 1-inch chunks (about 3 cups)

3 or 4 medium carrots, cut into 2-inch pieces (about 3 cups)

1 cup water

½ large head cabbage, chopped (5 to 6 cups)

Freshly ground black pepper

Salt (optional)

1. Select the Sauté function on your Instant Pot. Sauté the onion for 3 minutes, adding water as needed to prevent sticking. Add the ginger, paprika, cumin, and turmeric and stir for 30 seconds, until fragrant. Stir in the potatoes and carrots. Cancel the Sauté function. Pour in the water, stirring well. Place the cabbage on top but do not stir.

2. Lock the lid and turn the steam release handle to Sealing. Using the Pressure Cook/Manual function, set the cooker to High Pressure for 2 minutes.

3. When the cook time is complete, quick-release the pressure and carefully remove the lid. Stir and season to taste with pepper and salt (if using). Serve immediately. Store any leftovers in the fridge for up to 4 days in a covered container.

VARIATION TIP: Change up the spices for different flavors. Replace the turmeric, paprika, and cumin with garlic powder and Italian seasoning and add plant-based Italian sausage for a more Mediterranean flair, or use vegan kielbasa seasoned with garlic powder and fennel for the flavors of Eastern Europe.

PER SERVING: Calories: 186; Fat: 1g; Protein: 6g; Total Carbs: 42g; Fiber: 8g; Sugar: 8g; Sodium: 64mg

Classic Plant-Based Lasagna

WFPB **ONE-POT MEAL** **WORTH THE WAIT**

PREP TIME: 15 minutes **COOK SETTING:** High Pressure for 20 minutes **RELEASE:** Natural for 10 minutes, then quick **TOTAL TIME:** 1 hour, plus 30 to 45 minutes for resting

I was dubious I could make lasagna in the Instant Pot, but I am thrilled to report this recipe came out perfectly. It's made in a smaller pan than a typical lasagna, so don't plan on any leftovers. **Serves 4**

1 (14-ounce) package firm tofu, drained

2 tablespoons unsweetened plant-based milk

Juice from ½ lemon

2 tablespoons nutritional yeast

1 teaspoon garlic powder

1 teaspoon no-salt-added Italian seasoning

Freshly ground black pepper

Salt (optional)

2 cups Oil-Free Marinara Sauce (page 109) or store-bought

6 to 9 no-boil whole-grain lasagna noodles

1 (10-ounce) package frozen spinach, thawed and squeezed dry

1½ cups water

1. In a blender or food processor, combine the tofu, milk, lemon juice, nutritional yeast, garlic powder, and Italian seasoning and season to taste with pepper and salt (if using). Blend well.

2. In a 7-inch springform pan, pour ⅓ cup of the sauce. Top with a layer of lasagna noodles, breaking them to fit. Then layer ⅓ cup of sauce, followed by a third of the tofu mixture, a third of the spinach, and another layer of noodles. Repeat layering in this pattern until all the ingredients are used, ending with a final layer of sauce.

3. Cover the pan tightly with aluminum foil. Pour the water into your Instant Pot and insert the trivet. Place the pan on the trivet. Lock the lid and turn the steam release handle to Sealing. Using the Pressure Cook/Manual function, set the cooker to High Pressure for 20 minutes.

4. When the cook time is complete, let the pressure release naturally for 10 minutes; quick-release any remaining pressure and carefully remove the lid. Remove the pan, keep covered, and let rest for 30 to 45 minutes before slicing and serving.

INGREDIENT TIP: In a pinch, you can substitute farfalle for the lasagna noodles.

PER SERVING: Calories: 395; Fat: 10g; Protein: 28g; Total Carbs: 57g; Fiber: 11g; Sugar: 5g; Sodium: 85mg

Lemon Cheezecake, page 104

CHAPTER 7
Desserts

Chocolate and Banana Steel-Cut Oatmeal

GLUTEN-FREE WFPB 5 OR FEWER INGREDIENTS QUICK

PREP TIME: 5 minutes **COOK SETTING:** High Pressure for 10 minutes **RELEASE:** Natural for 10 minutes, then quick **TOTAL TIME:** 30 minutes

Pop this in your Instant Pot while you clean the kitchen after dinner and you'll have a hot, decadent, and chocolatey dessert waiting for you when you're finished. If you decide to eat this for breakfast, I won't tell! **Serves 4 to 6**

5 medium bananas, divided

4 cups water

2 cups gluten-free steel-cut oats

1 cup unsweetened plant-based milk, plus more (optional) for serving

3 tablespoons cocoa powder

6 tablespoons maple syrup

VARIATION TIP: For a Mexican-style version, stir in 1 teaspoon each of pure vanilla extract and ground cinnamon before cooking. For a dessert kids of all ages will enjoy, add a heaping tablespoon of peanut butter and a tablespoon or two of dairy-free chocolate chips to each serving.

1. In a small bowl, mash 2 of the bananas and set aside. In your Instant Pot, whisk together the water, oats, milk, and cocoa powder. Add the mashed bananas on top but do not stir. Lock the lid and turn the steam release handle to Sealing. Using the Pressure Cook/Manual function, set the cooker to High Pressure for 10 minutes.

2. When the cook time is complete, let the pressure release naturally for 10 minutes; quick-release any remaining pressure and carefully remove the lid. Add the maple syrup, stir well to incorporate, and divide the oatmeal among serving bowls. Slice the remaining 3 bananas and top each bowl of oatmeal with bananas and a few tablespoons of milk (if desired). Serve immediately. Store leftovers in the fridge for up to 4 days in a covered container. The oatmeal will thicken in the fridge but will loosen up when you reheat it in the microwave or on the stovetop over medium heat.

PER SERVING: Calories: 583; Fat: 9g; Protein: 12g; Total Carbs: 120g; Fiber: 13g; Sugar: 40g; Sodium: 36mg

Cider-Poached Pears

GLUTEN-FREE **NUT-FREE** **SOY-FREE** **WFPB** **QUICK**

PREP TIME: 5 minutes **COOK SETTING:** High Pressure for 8 minutes, Sauté for 5 to 7 minutes **RELEASE:** Quick **TOTAL TIME:** 30 minutes

Poached pears make an elegant dessert. Red wine is often used for poaching; however, this cider version is every bit as delicious. For a more rustic feel, you can serve the hot spiced cider in mugs alongside the pears for a tasty beverage. **Serves 4 to 6**

4 to 6 D'Anjou pears, peeled

5 cups apple cider

3 cinnamon sticks

3 star anise pods

Dairy-free chocolate, melted (optional)

4 to 6 mint sprigs, for serving (optional)

1. In your Instant Pot, combine the pears, cider, cinnamon, and star anise. Lock the lid and turn the steam release handle to Sealing. Using the Pressure Cook/Manual function, set the cooker to High Pressure for 8 minutes.

2. When the cook time is complete, quick-release the pressure and carefully remove the lid. Remove the pears to warmed shallow serving bowls and set aside. Select the Sauté function, bring the cider to a boil, then reduce the sauce for 5 to 7 minutes. Ladle ¼ cup of the cider sauce into each serving bowl.

3. If desired, top each serving with a drizzle of chocolate and a mint sprig.

4. Store the pears submerged in the cider in the fridge for up to 1 day. Reheat in a saucepan or in the Instant Pot using the Sauté function.

INGREDIENT TIP: I tested this recipe using several common varieties of pears and found D'Anjou to be the best. As they poach, they become soft and creamy, whereas other varieties get slightly gritty and take longer to cook.

PER SERVING: Calories: 244; Fat: 1g; Protein: 1g; Total Carbs: 62g; Fiber: 6g; Sugar: 47g; Sodium: 14mg

Sweet Potato Spice Cake

NUT-FREE **SOY-FREE** **WORTH THE WAIT**

PREP TIME: 15 minutes **COOK SETTING:** High Pressure for 50 minutes **RELEASE:** Natural
TOTAL TIME: 1 hour 30 minutes

By grating the raw sweet potatoes, you end up with a perfectly moist cake. The orange juice, dates, and applesauce all lend a sweetness that is perfectly balanced by the warm spices. **Serves 4 to 6**

2 tablespoons ground flaxseed

1¾ cups water, divided

1½ cups white whole wheat flour

¾ teaspoon baking soda

¾ teaspoon baking powder

2½ teaspoons pumpkin pie spice

¼ teaspoon salt

1 cup orange juice

6 whole pitted dates

¼ cup Simple Applesauce (page 114) or no-sugar-added store-bought

1 cup peeled, grated sweet potatoes (about 1 medium)

Nonstick spray

FLAVOR BOOST: Create a maple glaze using ½ cup of confectioners' sugar mixed with ¼ cup of maple syrup. Drizzle over the cake just before serving.

1. In a small bowl, stir together the flaxseed and ¼ cup of the water. Set aside.

2. In a medium bowl, whisk together the flour, baking soda, baking powder, pumpkin pie spice, and salt.

3. In a blender, puree the orange juice and dates. Pour the mixture over the dry ingredients. Add the applesauce and flaxseed mixture and mix until just moistened. Stir in the sweet potatoes. Spray a 6-inch cake pan with nonstick spray and pour and spread the batter evenly. Cover tightly with aluminum foil.

4. Pour the remaining 1½ cups of water into your Instant Pot and insert the trivet. Place the cake pan on the trivet. Lock the lid and turn the steam release handle to Sealing. Using the Pressure Cook/Manual function, set the cooker to High Pressure for 50 minutes.

5. When the cook time is complete, let the pressure release naturally and carefully remove the lid. Remove the cake pan, remove the foil, and let cool for 5 minutes before turning out the cake on a cooling rack to cool completely. Store leftover cake in the fridge for up to 2 days.

PER SERVING: Calories: 269; Fat: 3g; Protein: 8g; Total Carbs: 57g; Fiber: 8g; Sugar: 15g; Sodium: 408mg

Blueberry Cobbler

GLUTEN-FREE **SOY-FREE** **QUICK**

PREP TIME: 10 minutes **COOK SETTING:** High Pressure for 7 minutes **RELEASE:** Quick
TOTAL TIME: 30 minutes

Each July when my girls were growing up, we would go blueberry picking and bring home not only blueberries but also purple tongues that revealed just how much we sampled in the fields! Blueberries freeze well, and you can use either fresh or frozen in this recipe. Serves 4 to 6

¾ cup water

4 cups blueberries (fresh or frozen)

Zest and juice of 1 lemon

6 tablespoons maple syrup, divided

1 tablespoon arrowroot powder

1 cup gluten-free old-fashioned rolled oats

½ cup almond flour

½ cup shredded unsweetened coconut

¼ cup Simple Applesauce (page 114) or no-sugar-added store-bought

1 teaspoon ground cinnamon

1 teaspoon pure vanilla extract

2 tablespoons plant-based butter (optional)

FLAVOR BOOST: Serve this cobbler topped with banana ice cream. Simply blend frozen bananas with a splash of plant-based milk until creamy.

1. Pour the water into your Instant Pot and insert the trivet. In a large mixing bowl, slightly mash together the berries, lemon zest and juice, 2 tablespoons of the maple syrup, and the arrowroot, keeping some berries intact. Pour the berry mixture into a 6-inch baking dish.

2. In a medium bowl, stir together the oats, almond flour, coconut, applesauce, cinnamon, vanilla, the remaining 4 tablespoons of maple syrup, and the butter (if using). Spread the topping over the blueberry mixture. Create a foil sling by folding a long piece of aluminum foil in half vertically two times; then use it to lower the baking dish into the pot. Lock the lid and turn the steam release handle to Sealing. Using the Pressure Cook/Manual function, set the cooker to High Pressure for 7 minutes.

3. When the cook time is complete, quick-release the pressure and carefully remove the lid. Remove the pan and, if desired, place it under a broiler for 30 to 60 seconds to brown the topping. Serve immediately. Store leftovers in a covered container at room temperature for up to 1 day.

PER SERVING: Calories: 364; Fat: 11g; Protein: 7g; Total Carbs: 64g; Fiber: 9g; Sugar: 36g; Sodium: 10mg

Decadent Chocolate Cake

GLUTEN-FREE **WORTH THE WAIT**

PREP TIME: 10 minutes **COOK SETTING:** Slow Cook for 1 hour 30 minutes
RELEASE: Natural **TOTAL TIME:** 1 hour 50 minutes

I almost called this recipe "perfect" chocolate cake, because that's how it came out—perfectly! If you love a rich, moist, and decadent chocolate cake, this may become your go-to. **Serves 4 to 6**

1 cup unsweetened plant-based milk

1½ teaspoons ground flaxseed

1½ teaspoons apple cider vinegar

2 teaspoons pure vanilla extract

¾ cup gluten-free flour blend

⅔ cup pure cane sugar

⅔ cup cocoa powder

¼ cup almond flour

½ teaspoon baking powder

¼ teaspoon baking soda

Pinch of salt

Nonstick cooking spray

1½ cups water

1. In a medium bowl, stir together the milk, flaxseed, vinegar, and vanilla. Set aside.

2. In a large bowl, whisk together the flour blend, sugar, cocoa powder, almond flour, baking powder, baking soda, and salt. Add the wet ingredients to the dry ingredients, stirring until just combined.

3. Spray a 6-inch cake pan with nonstick spray. Spread the batter evenly into the pan. Cover the pan tightly with aluminum foil.

4. Pour the water into your Instant Pot and insert the trivet. Place the cake pan on the trivet. Lock the lid and turn the steam release handle to Venting. Set the Slow Cook function to High for 1 hour 30 minutes.

5. When the cook time is complete, carefully remove the lid. After the steam subsides, remove the cake pan and set on a cooling rack for 10 minutes before turning it out. Let cool completely on the rack before serving.

FLAVOR BOOST: Create a ganache frosting by combining a ½ cup vegan chocolate chips and 2 tablespoons plant-based milk in a microwave-safe bowl and microwaving in 30-second increments, stirring after each, until melted and smooth. Spread over the top of the cooled cake.

PER SERVING: Calories: 320; Fat: 8g; Protein: 8g; Total Carbs: 61g; Fiber: 7g; Sugar: 28g; Sodium: 158mg

Millet Vanilla Pudding

GLUTEN-FREE **WFPB** **5 OR FEWER INGREDIENTS** **QUICK**

PREP TIME: 5 minutes **COOK SETTING:** High Pressure for 15 minutes **RELEASE:** Natural
TOTAL TIME: 30 minutes

Millet is a fine grain, and this easy dish tastes like a delicious cross between rice pudding and tapioca pudding. Be sure to add the maple syrup at the end to avoid a burn notice while it cooks. I like to serve this dessert with a dollop of coconut cream and a few fresh berries on top. **Serves 4 to 6**

2 cups water

1½ cups unsweetened plant-based milk, plus more for serving

1 cup millet

2 teaspoons pure vanilla extract

¼ cup maple syrup

1. In your Instant Pot, whisk together the water, milk, millet, and vanilla. Lock the lid and turn the steam release handle to Sealing. Using the Pressure Cook/Manual function, set the cooker to High Pressure for 15 minutes.

2. When the cook time is complete, let the pressure release naturally and carefully remove the lid. Add the maple syrup and stir well to incorporate. Serve warm immediately, or chill for 3 to 4 hours and serve cold. The pudding will become thicker as it cools. Store in the fridge for up to 4 days in a covered container.

INGREDIENT TIP: Millet tends to go rancid if stored for too long after packaging. Be sure to select a package with an expiration date far in the future. You'll know if your millet has turned because it has a bitter aftertaste when cooked.

PER SERVING: Calories: 284; Fat: 4g; Protein: 8g; Total Carbs: 53g; Fiber: 5g; Sugar: 14g; Sodium: 50mg

Lemon Cheezecake

GLUTEN-FREE **SOY-FREE** **WFPB** **WORTH THE WAIT**

PREP TIME: 20 minutes **COOK SETTING:** High Pressure for 25 minutes **RELEASE:** Natural
TOTAL TIME: 50 minutes, plus 6 hours for chilling

This recipe gets a star of approval from my dessert-loving father-in-law. The texture of this cheezecake is spot-on thanks to the secret ingredient: chickpeas. **Serves 6 to 8**

4 pitted dates

1½ cups walnuts

2 cups raw cashews, soaked in boiling water for 20 minutes

1 cup cooked chickpeas, drained and rinsed

½ cup maple syrup

2 tablespoons tahini

2 tablespoons apple cider vinegar

Zest and juice of 2 lemons

1 (13.5-ounce) can full-fat coconut milk

2 tablespoons arrowroot powder

½ teaspoon salt (optional)

1½ cups water

Lemon slices, for garnish

VARIATION TIP: Use any combination of walnuts, almonds, and pecans for the crust. Serve drizzled with Strawberry Compote (page 115).

1. Cover the dates with hot water and soak for 10 minutes. Drain, reserving the soaking water, roughly chop the dates, and add them to a food processor with the walnuts. Blend until sticky, adding a few drops of the reserved soaking liquid as needed. Press firmly into the bottom of a non-stick 7-inch springform pan. Set aside.

2. In a blender or food processor, combine the cashews, chickpeas, maple syrup, tahini, vinegar, and lemon zest and juice. Blend until smooth. Add the milk, arrowroot, and salt (if using). Blend to combine.

3. Pour the filling into the crust. Cover the pan tightly with aluminum foil. Pour the water into your Instant Pot and insert the trivet. Place the pan on the trivet. Lock the lid and turn the steam release handle to Sealing. Using the Pressure Cook/Manual function, set the cooker to High Pressure for 25 minutes.

4. When the cook time is complete, let the pressure release naturally and carefully remove the lid. Remove the pan, then the foil, and cool for 30 minutes before turning out onto a serving platter. Garnish with lemon slices. Chill at least 6 hours before serving.

PER SERVING: Calories: 745; Fat: 57g; Protein: 18g; Total Carbs: 53g; Fiber: 7g; Sugar: 24g; Sodium: 26mg

Apple Spice Cake

GLUTEN-FREE | **NUT-FREE** | **SOY-FREE** | **WORTH THE WAIT**

PREP TIME: 20 minutes **COOK SETTING:** High Pressure for 55 minutes **RELEASE:** Natural
TOTAL TIME: 1 hour 30 minutes

When I was a little girl, my great-aunt used to make a delicious apple spice cake, and this recipe takes me right back to those days. **Serves 4 to 6**

2 tablespoons ground flaxseed

5 tablespoons water, plus 1½ cups

3 medium apples, peeled, cored, and diced

3 teaspoons apple pie spice, divided

1 tablespoon maple syrup, plus ½ cup

1 cup gluten-free flour blend

1 cup gluten-free oat flour

2 teaspoons baking powder

½ teaspoon salt

1 cup Simple Applesauce (page 114) or no-sugar-added store-bought

1 teaspoon pure vanilla extract

Nonstick cooking spray

INGREDIENT TIP: Make your own apple pie spice by mixing 1 tablespoon of ground cinnamon and 1 teaspoon each of grated nutmeg, ground ginger, ground allspice, and ground cardamom.

1. In a small bowl, stir together the flaxseed and the 5 tablespoons of water. Set aside.

2. In a medium bowl, toss the apples with 2 teaspoons of the apple pie spice and 1 tablespoon of the maple syrup. In a large bowl, whisk together the flour blend, oat flour, baking powder, salt, and the remaining 1 teaspoon of apple pie spice.

3. In a medium bowl, whisk together the applesauce, vanilla, flax mixture, and the remaining ½ cup of maple syrup. Pour the wet ingredients into the dry and mix well.

4. Spray a 7-inch cake pan with nonstick cooking spray. Pour and spread half the batter into the pan. Top with half the apples. Repeat with the remaining batter and apples. Cover tightly with aluminum foil.

5. Pour the remaining 1½ cups of water into your Instant Pot and insert the trivet. Place the cake pan on the trivet. Lock and seal the lid. Set the cooker to High Pressure for 55 minutes.

6. When the cook time is complete, let the pressure release naturally and carefully remove the lid. Cool for 5 minutes before turning out onto a cooling rack to cool completely.

PER SERVING: Calories: 486; Fat: 5g; Protein: 8g; Total Carbs: 106g; Fiber: 9g; Sugar: 48g; Sodium: 310mg

Hot Pepper Sauce, page 112

CHAPTER 8
Sauces and Staples

Easy Vegetable Broth

GLUTEN-FREE **NUT-FREE** **SOY-FREE** **WFPB** **WORTH THE WAIT**

PREP TIME: 7 minutes **COOK SETTING:** Sauté for 3 to 5 minutes, High Pressure for 40 minutes **RELEASE:** Quick **TOTAL TIME:** 55 minutes

Typical broth can take hours, bubbling away on the stove, but with your Instant Pot, you can have a rich, full-flavored broth in less than an hour. To be economical, I make my broth from leftover veggie scraps that I store in a plastic bag in the freezer. *Makes 3 quarts*

2 medium onions, halved

2 celery stalks with leaves, roughly chopped

2 large carrots, scrubbed and roughly chopped

8 ounces white button or cremini mushrooms, whole

12 cups water

1 head garlic, halved crosswise

1 bunch parsley stems

2 bay leaves

5 to 7 whole black peppercorns

1. Select the Sauté function on your Instant Pot. Sauté the onions, celery, carrots, and mushrooms for 3 to 5 minutes, until slightly browned, adding water as needed to prevent sticking.

2. Add the water, garlic, parsley, bay leaves, and peppercorns. Lock the lid and turn the steam release handle to Sealing. Using the Pressure Cook/Manual function, set the cooker to High Pressure for 40 minutes.

3. When the cook time is complete, quick-release the pressure and carefully remove the lid. Strain the broth through a fine-mesh sieve into a large bowl and discard the solids. Store the broth in a covered container in the fridge for up to 4 days or in the freezer for up to 6 months.

FLAVOR BOOST: To bring more umami flavor to your broth, add 2 to 3 ounces of dried mushrooms, either shiitake or a blend. Season with 1 to 2 tablespoons of gluten-free soy sauce or coconut aminos.

PER SERVING (½ CUP): Calories: 10; Fat: 0g; Protein: 0g; Total Carbs: 2g; Fiber: 0g; Sugar: 0g; Sodium: 5mg

Oil-Free Marinara Sauce

GLUTEN-FREE NUT-FREE SOY-FREE WFPB

PREP TIME: 5 minutes **COOK SETTING:** Sauté for 1 to 2 minutes, High Pressure for 12 minutes **RELEASE:** Natural **TOTAL TIME:** 40 minutes

A good marinara sauce is worth its weight in gold. This version is bright, fresh, and seasoned the way my Italian grandmother used to season hers, with the added bonus that it's fat-free with zero oil. *Buon appetito!* **Makes about 6 cups**

1 medium onion, diced

4 tablespoons water, as needed

4 garlic cloves, minced

1 tablespoon dried basil

1 tablespoon dried oregano

¼ to 1 teaspoon red pepper flakes

2 (28-ounce) cans no-salt-added crushed tomatoes

½ cup Easy Vegetable Broth (page 108) or no-salt-added vegetable broth

Freshly ground black pepper

Salt (optional)

1. Select the Sauté function on your Instant Pot. Sauté the onion for 1 to 2 minutes, until slightly browned, adding water as needed to prevent sticking. Add the garlic, basil, oregano, and red pepper flakes to taste and stir for 30 seconds, until fragrant.

2. Stir in the tomatoes and broth, scraping up any browned bits from the bottom of the pot. Season to taste with black pepper and salt (if using). Lock the lid and turn the steam release handle to Sealing. Using the Pressure Cook/Manual function, set the cooker to High Pressure for 12 minutes.

3. When the cook time is complete, let the pressure release naturally and carefully remove the lid. Use immediately or store in a covered container in the fridge for up to 4 weeks or in the freezer for up to 3 months.

FLAVOR BOOST: Substitute red wine for the broth for a deeper, richer flavor. For a meatier texture, finely dice 8 ounces of fresh button or cremini mushrooms and sauté with the onions.

PER SERVING (½ CUP): Calories: 27; Fat: 0g; Protein: 1g; Total Carbs: 6g; Fiber: 3g; Sugar: 3g; Sodium: 14mg

Sweet and Tangy Maple Barbecue Sauce

GLUTEN-FREE **NUT-FREE** **SOY-FREE** **WFPB** **QUICK**

PREP TIME: 5 minutes **COOK SETTING:** Sauté for 2 minutes, High Pressure for 4 minutes **RELEASE:** Quick **TOTAL TIME:** 30 minutes

Use this barbecue sauce for the Kansas City–Style Barbecue Beans (page 75), in the Quick Barbecue Chili (page 58), stirred into cooked brown rice for a tangy side dish, or for anything you like. **Makes about 3 cups**

2 tablespoons minced onion

2 garlic cloves, minced

1 teaspoon smoked paprika

1 teaspoon ground allspice

1 cup water

1 (15-ounce) can no-salt-added tomato sauce

¼ cup maple syrup

2 tablespoons stone-ground mustard

2 tablespoons apple cider vinegar

½ teaspoon salt (optional)

VARIATION TIP: Experiment with additional spices and seasonings until you reach your perfect barbecue sauce. Use orange or pineapple juice in place of the water. Try adding mustard powder, ginger, vegan Worcestershire sauce, chili powder, or any other flavorings you like.

1. Select the Sauté function on your Instant Pot. Sauté the onion for 2 minutes, adding water as needed to prevent sticking, until slightly browned. Add the garlic, paprika, and allspice and stir for 30 seconds, until fragrant. Stir in the water, scraping up any browned bits from the bottom of the pot. Add the tomato sauce, maple syrup, mustard, vinegar, and salt (if using). Whisk to combine. Lock the lid and turn the steam release handle to Sealing. Using the Pressure Cook/Manual function, set the cooker to High Pressure for 4 minutes.

2. When the cook time is complete, quick-release the pressure and carefully remove the lid. If the sauce is not thick enough for your taste, select the Sauté function and allow the sauce to reduce, stirring frequently, until it reaches your desired consistency. Store in the fridge for up to 4 weeks in a covered container.

PER SERVING (¼ CUP): Calories: 26; Fat: 0g; Protein: 0g; Total Carbs: 6g; Fiber: 1g; Sugar: 5g; Sodium: 33mg

Fresh Tomato Ketchup

GLUTEN-FREE **NUT-FREE** **SOY-FREE** **WFPB** **QUICK**

PREP TIME: 5 minutes **COOK SETTING:** High Pressure for 5 minutes, Sauté for 10 minutes **RELEASE:** Quick **TOTAL TIME:** 30 minutes

I remember being blown away the first time I ever tasted homemade ketchup. This recipe is made from whole, plant-based ingredients and tastes so much better than any store-bought ketchup I've ever had. **Makes about 4 cups**

2 pounds plum tomatoes, roughly chopped

5 pitted dates

6 tablespoons distilled white vinegar

1 tablespoon gluten-free vegan Worcestershire sauce

1 tablespoon paprika

1 teaspoon onion powder

1 teaspoon salt (optional)

½ teaspoon mustard powder

¼ teaspoon celery seed

¼ teaspoon garlic powder

Pinch of ground cloves

2 tablespoons water

1 tablespoon arrowroot powder or cornstarch

1. In your Instant Pot, combine the tomatoes, dates, vinegar, Worcestershire sauce, paprika, onion powder, salt (if using), mustard powder, celery seed, garlic powder, and cloves. Using a potato masher, mash the tomatoes until they have released much of their liquid. Lock the lid and turn the steam release handle to Sealing. Using the Pressure Cook/Manual function, set the cooker to High Pressure for 5 minutes.

2. When the cook time is complete, quick-release the pressure and carefully remove the lid. Select the Sauté function and simmer about 10 minutes, until reduced, stirring often. In a small bowl, whisk together the water and arrowroot and add to the simmering ketchup, stirring until thickened, 2 to 4 minutes more. Strain the ketchup through a fine-mesh sieve. The ketchup will thicken as it cools. Store in the fridge for up to 6 months in a covered container.

INGREDIENT TIP: I recommend plum tomatoes for this recipe because their ratio of liquid to pulp yields just the right texture for this ketchup.

PER SERVING (1 TABLESPOON): Calories: 6; Fat: 0g; Protein: 0g; Total Carbs: 1g; Fiber: 0g; Sugar: 1g; Sodium: 40mg

Hot Pepper Sauce

GLUTEN-FREE **NUT-FREE** **SOY-FREE** **WFPB** **5 OR FEWER INGREDIENTS** **QUICK**

PREP TIME: 3 minutes **COOK SETTING:** High Pressure for 2 minutes **RELEASE:** Natural
TOTAL TIME: 30 minutes

Most commercially available hot sauces contain salt. This version is a simple whole food, plant-based recipe without any added salt, and your taste buds won't miss it! Sprinkle it over anything that needs a spicy kick, such as Breakfast Potatoes, Onions, and Peppers (page 23) or Southwestern Taco Bowls (page 80). **Makes about 1¾ cups**

12 to 16 ounces fresh hot red peppers, stems removed, halved

1 cup distilled white vinegar

¼ cup apple cider vinegar

3 garlic cloves, smashed

1. In your Instant Pot, stir together the peppers, white vinegar, cider vinegar, and garlic. Lock the lid and turn the steam release handle to Sealing. Using the Pressure Cook/Manual function, set the cooker to High Pressure for 2 minutes.

2. When the cook time is complete, let the pressure release naturally and carefully remove the lid, keeping your face away from the steam, which, depending on the spiciness of the peppers, can burn your sinuses. Using an immersion blender, food processor, or blender, blend the sauce until smooth. Strain through a fine-mesh sieve and store in glass bottles or jars at room temperature for up to 6 months.

INGREDIENT TIP: When you make your own hot pepper sauce, you get to choose the level of spiciness. Choose hot peppers based on the amount of heat you enjoy. Feel free to use milder green peppers like jalapeños or serranos, a super-hot Scotch bonnet pepper, or a mix of peppers to achieve your perfect blend.

PER SERVING (1 TEASPOON): Calories: 3; Fat: 0g; Protein: 0g; Total Carbs: 1g; Fiber: 0g; Sugar: 0g; Sodium: 1mg

Nut-Free Cheeze Sauce

GLUTEN-FREE **NUT-FREE** **SOY-FREE** **WFPB** **QUICK**

PREP TIME: 5 minutes **COOK SETTING:** High Pressure for 7 minutes **RELEASE:** Natural for 10 minutes, then quick **TOTAL TIME:** 30 minutes

I love a good cheesy sauce as much as anyone, and this recipe is easy to make with basics you likely have on hand right now. Not only is it nut-free, but it is also fat-free. Yet it is every bit as creamy as the real thing thanks to the starch in the potatoes. **Makes about 2 cups**

- 3 medium yellow potatoes, cut into 1-inch chunks
- 1 large carrot, cut into 1-inch chunks
- 2 cups water
- ¼ cup nutritional yeast
- 2 tablespoons freshly squeezed lemon juice
- 2 teaspoons chickpea miso paste
- ½ teaspoon onion powder
- ½ teaspoon garlic powder
- ½ teaspoon mustard powder
- ¼ teaspoon ground turmeric

1. In your Instant Pot, combine the potatoes, carrot, and water. Lock the lid and turn the steam release handle to Sealing. Using the Pressure Cook/Manual function, set the cooker to High Pressure for 7 minutes.

2. When the cook time is complete, let the pressure release naturally for 10 minutes; quick-release any remaining pressure and carefully remove the lid. Using a slotted spoon, remove the potatoes and carrots to a blender, then add ½ cup of the cooking water along with the nutritional yeast, lemon juice, miso, onion powder, garlic powder, mustard powder, and turmeric. Blend until smooth and creamy, adding more cooking water as necessary to thin. Store in the fridge for up to 4 days in a covered container.

LEFTOVERS TIP: Use this cheeze sauce on everything from nachos to baked potatoes. Mix it with rice and steamed broccoli for a quick and easy meal.

PER SERVING (¼ CUP): Calories: 123; Fat: 0g; Protein: 4g; Total Carbs: 26g; Fiber: 4g; Sugar: 2g; Sodium: 72mg

Simple Applesauce

GLUTEN-FREE **NUT-FREE** **SOY-FREE** **WFPB** **5 OR FEWER INGREDIENTS** **QUICK**

PREP TIME: 10 minutes **COOK SETTING:** High Pressure for 4 minutes **RELEASE:** Natural for 10 minutes, then quick **TOTAL TIME:** 30 minutes

Applesauce is such a staple in my house that I just had to include it here. My younger daughter loves it in her lunch box, and I like to use it in baking recipes to replace oil and add natural sweetness. When you choose sweet varieties of apples such as Gala or Fuji, adding sugar isn't necessary. And there's no need to peel the apples; it's faster to pluck out the peels at the end, blend them, and add them back to the applesauce for the perfect texture. **Makes about 4 cups**

3 pounds apples, cored, cut into large chunks

⅓ cup water

1 tablespoon freshly squeezed lemon juice

1. In your Instant Pot, combine the apples, water, and lemon juice. Lock the lid and turn the steam release handle to Sealing. Using the Pressure Cook/Manual function, set the cooker to High Pressure for 4 minutes.

2. When the cook time is complete, let the pressure release naturally for 10 minutes; quick-release any remaining pressure and carefully remove the lid. Using a potato masher, mash the apples to your desired chunkiness. Using a pair of tongs or a fork, transfer the apple peels to a deep, narrow container and blend using an immersion blender. Return to the pot and stir to combine. Store in the fridge for up to 4 weeks in a covered container.

FLAVOR BOOST: If you like cinnamon in your applesauce, add a teaspoon after cooking and be ready—the whole batch will turn a light-brown color. To preserve the apple color, I prefer to sprinkle a bit of cinnamon on each serving instead.

PER SERVING (½ CUP): Calories: 89; Fat: 0g; Protein: 0g; Total Carbs: 24g; Fiber: 4g; Sugar: 18g; Sodium: 2mg

Strawberry Compote

GLUTEN-FREE NUT-FREE SOY-FREE 5 OR FEWER INGREDIENTS QUICK

PREP TIME: 3 minutes **COOK SETTING:** High Pressure for 4 minutes **RELEASE:** Natural for 10 minutes, then quick **TOTAL TIME:** 30 minutes

There are a couple of surprising things about this recipe. First, it's made from readily available frozen berries, so you don't have to wait for strawberry season. Second, it's made without any water; the natural juices of the strawberries combined with the sugar and lemon juice yield plenty of liquid to avoid a burn notice. Use this compote as a topping for Lemon Cheezecake (page 104), a mix-in for Soy Yogurt (page 21), or however you like! **Makes about 2 cups**

4 cups frozen strawberries (28 ounces)

¼ cup sugar

1 tablespoon freshly squeezed lemon juice

1. In your Instant Pot, combine the strawberries, sugar, and lemon juice. Stir to coat the berries. Lock the lid and turn the steam release handle to Sealing. Using the Pressure Cook/Manual function, set the cooker to High Pressure for 4 minutes.

2. When the cook time is complete, let the pressure release naturally for 10 minutes; quick-release any remaining pressure and carefully remove the lid. Using a potato masher, mash the berries until they are broken down completely. Pour into a container and chill. The compote will thicken as it cools. Store in the fridge for up to 4 weeks in a covered container.

VARIATION TIP: If you'd like to use fresh berries, reduce the cooking time to 2 minutes. Use any combination of berries you like.

PER SERVING (1 TABLESPOON): Calories: 16; Fat: 0g; Protein: 0g; Total Carbs: 4g; Fiber: 1g; Sugar: 3g; Sodium: 1mg

Classic Plant-Based Lasagna, page 94

Measurement Conversions

Volume Equivalents (Liquid)

US STANDARD	US STANDARD (OUNCES)	METRIC (APPROXIMATE)
2 tablespoons	1 fl. oz.	30 mL
¼ cup	2 fl. oz.	60 mL
½ cup	4 fl. oz.	120 mL
1 cup	8 fl. oz.	240 mL
1 ½ cups	12 fl. oz.	355 mL
2 cups or 1 pint	16 fl. oz.	475 mL
4 cups or 1 quart	32 fl. oz.	1 L
1 gallon	128 fl. oz.	4 L

Oven Temperatures

FAHRENHEIT	CELSIUS (APPROXIMATE)
250°F	120°C
300°F	150°C
325°F	165°C
350°F	180°C
375°F	190°C
400°F	200°C
425°F	220°C
450°F	230°C

Volume Equivalents (Dry)

US STANDARD	METRIC (APPROXIMATE)
⅛ teaspoon	0.5 mL
¼ teaspoon	1 mL
½ teaspoon	2 mL
¾ teaspoon	4 mL
1 teaspoon	5 mL
1 tablespoon	15 mL
¼ cup	59 mL
⅓ cup	79 mL
½ cup	118 mL
⅔ cup	156 mL
¾ cup	177 mL
1 cup	235 mL
2 cups or 1 pint	475 mL
3 cups	700 mL
4 cups or 1 quart	1 L

Weight Equivalents

US STANDARD	METRIC (APPROXIMATE)
½ ounce	15 g
1 ounce	30 g
2 ounces	60 g
4 ounces	115 g
8 ounces	225 g
12 ounces	340 g
16 ounces or 1 pound	455 g

References

Alexander, Heather. "5 Benefits of a Plant-Based Diet." MD Anderson Cancer Center. November 2019. MDAnderson.org/publications/focused-on -health/5-benefits-of-a-plant-based-diet.h20-1592991.html.

Blankenhorn, D. H., R. L. Johnson, W. J. Mack, H. A. el Zein, and L. I. Vailas. "The Influence of Diet on the Appearance of New Lesions in Human Coronary Arteries." *JAMA* 263 (12): 1646–52. PubMed.ncbi.nlm.nih.gov/2407875.

Campbell, T. Colin, and Thomas M. Campbell II. *The China Study: The Most Comprehensive Study of Nutrition Ever Conducted and the Startling Implications for Diet, Weight Loss and Long-term Health.* Dallas: Benbella Books, 2006.

Earthday.org. "UN Report: Plant-Based Diets Provide 'Major Opportunities' to Address Climate Crisis." August 8, 2019. EarthDay.org/un-report-plant -based-diets-provide-major-opportunities-to-address-climate-crisis.

Greger, Michael. *How Not to Die: Discover the Foods Scientifically Proven to Prevent and Reverse Disease.* New York: Flatiron Books, 2015.

———. *How Not to Diet: The Groundbreaking Science of Healthy, Permanent Weight Loss.* New York: Flatiron Books, 2019.

———. "Olive Oil & Artery Function." NutritionFacts.org. August 17, 2015. NutritionFacts.org/video/olive-oil-and-artery-function.

Harvard T. H. Chan School of Public Health. "Straight Talk About Soy." Accessed April 11, 2021. HSPH.harvard.edu/nutritionsource/soy.

Hudepohl, Dana. "How to Support Your Immune System with a Plant-Based Diet." Forks Over Knives. April 1, 2020. ForksOverKnives.com/wellness /immune-system-health-plant-based-diet.

Hunnes, Dana. "The Case for Plant Based." UCLA Sustainability. Accessed
    April 11, 2021. Sustain.ucla.edu/food-systems/the-case-for-plant-based.

Intergovernmental Panel on Climate Change. *Special Report on Climate
    Change and Land: Summary for Policymakers*. Accessed April 11, 2021.
    IPCC.ch/srccl/chapter/summary-for-policymakers.

National Academies of Sciences, Engineering, and Medicine. "Dietary Reference
    Intakes for Sodium and Potassium." March 2019. NAP.edu/resource/25353
    /030519DRISodiumPotassium.pdf.

Pahwa, Roma, Amandeep Goyal, Pankaj Bansal, and Ishwarlal Jialal. "Chronic
    Inflammation." *National Center for Biotechnology Information*. Last updated
    November 20, 2020. NCBI.nlm.nih.gov/books/NBK493173.

Vogel, Robert A., Mary C. Corretti, and Gary D. Plotnick. "The Postprandial
    Effect of Components of the Mediterranean Diet on Endothelial Function."
    Journal of the American College of Cardiology 36 (5): 1455–60,
    doi:10.1016/S0735-1097(00)00896-2.

Watzl, Bernhard. "Anti-inflammatory Effects of Plant-Based Foods and of
    Their Constituents." *International Journal for Vitamin and Nutrition
    Research* 78 (6): 293–8, doi:10.1024/0300-9831.78.6.293.

Index

Acknowledgments

Many hands make light work, and this, my second cookbook (and eighth book overall!), was one of the easiest I've written, thanks to so many people. To my editor, Marjorie DeWitt: Thank you for your helpful comments, your encouragement along the way, and your hard work in relieving my "Ack! Please help" moments. A big thanks to you, and to all the teams at Rockridge Press.

To my recipe testers, Erin Bush, Stephanie Callahan, Kirsten Kropilak, Lynette Montae, Beth Walls, Terri Ward, and Amy Wood: Thank you for jumping in and being willing to give my recipes a try exactly as they were written and sharing your honest thoughts and opinions. This book is better for your contributions.

To the members of my Plant-Based Home Cooking with Felicia Slattery Facebook group: Thank you for your excitement and willingness to try new foods, experimentation with new recipes and techniques, comments on and liking my posts, and for asking thoughtful questions and coming on your own plant-based journey with me.

To my mom, Joan Slattery, and my in-laws, Anne and Richard Parkhill: Thank you for enthusiastically tasting my food, along with your love and encouragement, as well as being my teachers in the kitchen.

Finally, and above all, I give thanks and glory to God for setting in motion the steps in Your plan for this part of my life decades ago, and for putting the right people in my path to get me to where I am today.

About the Author

 **Felicia Slattery** is an award-winning home cook who began her adventures in the kitchen at a young age. She took every cooking class her high school offered, worked in restaurants through college and beyond, and took cooking classes at Le Cordon Bleu in Paris. She is a popular food blogger as well as the creator of PlantBasedHomeCooking.com and the Facebook group and YouTube channel Plant-Based Home Cooking with Felicia Slattery, where she regularly shares her recipes and stories and helps others discover the joy of living a healthy plant-based lifestyle.